Mental Fitness for Young Rugby Players

Cole Levitt

MENTAL FITNESS
Series
for YOUNG ATHLETES

Mastering the Mental Game

@mentalfitnessforyoungathletes

Mental Fitness for Young Athletes

Mental Fitness for Young Athletes

TABLE OF CONTENTS

INTRODUCTION:
Building Mental Fitness for Young Rugby Players

In rugby, long-term success requires more than just physical strength, speed, and skill. It demands mental toughness, resilience, and the ability to adapt under pressure. As you step onto the field, the mental game becomes just as critical as the physical. This book is your guide to building the mental fitness needed to thrive in rugby, on the pitch—and beyond.

Rugby is a dynamic, fast-paced sport with some moments of intense physical contact, strategic decision-making, and the need for ongoing teamwork. Whether you're preparing for a match, facing a top-notch opponent, or recovering from an injury, your mindset can determine your performance and how you handle the challenges that come your way. Mental fitness equips you with the tools to stay calm and focused under pressure, bounce back from mistakes or losses, maintain confidence and composure in high-stakes situations, and foster strong communication and trust with teammates. In a game where the outcome often hinges on split-second decisions, the ability to control your thoughts, emotions, and actions becomes a game-changer.

What You'll Learn in This Book:

This book is designed to help you master the mental side of rugby. Each chapter looks into a key aspect of sports psychology, offering insights, strategies, and practical exercises to sharpen your mental skills. You will learn how to identify **mental blocks** that hold you back, such as fear of failure, self-doubt, or performance anxiety. Understanding these barriers is the first step toward breaking through them and unlocking your full potential on the field.

The book will explore **emotional regulation**, an essential skill in a sport as intense as rugby. High adrenaline, frustration, and excitement can affect your focus and decision-making, leading to knock-ons, poor passes, and missed tackles. Learning techniques such as deep breathing and emotional awareness will help you stay composed, no matter what happens during a game. You'll also discover the power of **visualization**, a technique used by top athletes to mentally rehearse plays, anticipate challenges, and boost confidence. By practicing visualization, you can prepare for the unexpected and strengthen your belief in your abilities.

Developing a **growth mindset** is another cornerstone of mental fitness. A growth mindset involves believing that your abilities can improve through effort and learning and that mistakes will happen and are part of the development process. This outlook is crucial for embracing challenges, learning from setbacks, and continually improving your skills. By building a positive and resilient mindset, you'll not only lift your performance but also inspire your teammates to do the same.

Resilience and grit are qualities every rugby player needs to navigate the highs and lows of the game and a season. Whether you're dealing with tough losses, physical injuries, or other setbacks, these traits enable you to persevere and keep pushing forward. This book will guide you through strategies to build these qualities, ensuring that you're ready to tackle any obstacle that comes your way.

Mindfulness, the practice of staying present and fully engaged in the moment, is another critical skill for rugby players. In a sport as unpredictable as rugby, mindfulness can enhance your awareness, reaction time, and ability to stay composed under pressure. You'll learn simple mindfulness practices tailored for athletes, helping you remain focused and perform at your best.

Goal setting is an essential tool that provides direction and purpose. By setting clear, actionable goals, you can chart a path toward success and measure your progress along the way. This book will introduce you to effective goal-setting techniques, such as defining process, performance, and outcome goals.

Positive self-talk is another necessary component of mental fitness. The way you talk to yourself matters, especially in high-pressure situations. Reframing negative thoughts and focusing on constructive, encouraging dialogue can boost your confidence, motivation, and overall performance. You'll learn how to harness the power of positive self-talk to stay optimistic and focused, even when faced with massive challenges.

Consistency breeds confidence, and developing **pre-game rituals** and routines is a key part of preparing for success. From warm-ups to mental checklists, creating a routine helps you get into the right mindset and reduce pre-match jitters. This book will help you design rituals and routines that work for you, ensuring you step onto the field feeling prepared and confident.

Performance reflection is an often overlooked aspect of growth. Taking the time to analyze your performance—both your successes and areas for improvement—is essential for continuous development. By reflecting constructively, you'll gain valuable insights into your game and learn how to apply those lessons moving forward.

Each chapter includes explanations of the mental skill being discussed, real-life examples from some of the biggest rugby legends, and activities for you to apply right away. These activities are designed to be engaging, practical, and tailored to your experiences as a young rugby player. By applying what you learn, you'll develop a personalized toolkit of mental strategies that you can use both on and off the field. It's important to approach this book with an open mind and a willingness to put in the effort. Mental fitness, like physical fitness, requires practice, many repetitions, and ongoing commitment. The more you engage with the exercises and reflect on your progress, the stronger your mental game will become.

Building mental fitness doesn't just benefit your rugby performance; it also prepares you for challenges in other areas of life. The skills you develop—resilience, focus, goal-setting, and self-awareness—are transferable to school, relationships, and future careers. Rugby may be the arena where you build these skills, but their impact will extend far beyond the field.

As you start your mental fitness journey, remember that mental fitness is a process. It's about growth, not perfection. Whether you're just picking up the game of rugby or looking to break into your club's top side, this book is here to guide you every step of the way. The mental edge you develop will not only enhance your performance but also deepen your love for the game.

So, lace up your boots, pop in your mouthguard, take a deep breath, and get ready to tackle the mental side of rugby. The pitch is yours to conquer—one mental skill at a time.

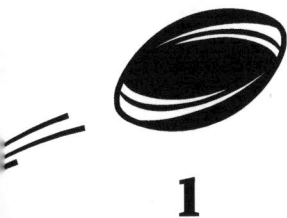

1

BREAKING THE LINE:
Identifying and Fending Off Mental Blocks

Learning to manage the mental side of rugby is as important as learning how to tackle, pass, or scrummage. Sometimes, players face challenges in their minds that hold them back. These challenges, called mental blocks, can make it hard to play confidently and freely. Mental blocks affect how players think and feel about their performance, and they can show up in many different ways. To be the best you can be on the rugby field, it's vital to understand what mental blocks are and how they can impact your game.

Types of Mental Blocks:

Fear of Failure
One of the most common mental blocks young rugby players experience is the fear of failure. This happens when a player becomes so focused on not making mistakes that it affects their performance. For example, you might worry about dropping the ball at a key moment or missing an important tackle. This fear often comes from putting too much pressure on yourself or feeling like you have to prove something to your coach, teammates, or even your family. Instead of enjoying the game and playing to your full ability, you may find yourself hesitating, playing too cautiously, or avoiding big plays. Fear of failure can make rugby feel more like a test than a sport, which can take away the fun and excitement of the game.

Overthinking

Rugby is a fast-paced sport where quick decisions can make the difference between winning and losing. Overthinking is a mental block that slows you down by making you question your instincts. You might find yourself hesitating as you decide whether to pass, kick, or run with the ball. Overthinking can also happen when you replay past mistakes in your head while the game is still happening. Instead of staying focused on the moment, your mind gets stuck on "What if?" scenarios or regrets about what just happened. Over time, overthinking can make you doubt your abilities and leave you feeling mentally drained during games.

Self-Doubt

Self-doubt is another mental block that many young rugby players face. This block is all about questioning whether you're good enough to succeed. You might wonder if you're as skilled as your teammates or if you even deserve to be on the team. These thoughts can creep in after a tough loss, a mistake on the field, or even if you compare yourself too much to others. Self-doubt doesn't just affect how you feel—it can also change how you play. Instead of going all-in on tackles or trying new moves, you might hold back because you're afraid of messing up. Self-doubt can take away the confidence you need to perform at your best.

Fear of Physical Contact

Rugby is known for its physical nature, and while some players thrive on the sport's intensity, others may struggle with a fear of contact. This mental block often comes from worries about getting hurt or not feeling strong enough to face physical challenges on the field. Fear of contact can make a player hesitate during tackles, shy away from rucks, or avoid situations where they need to be aggressive. Over time, this hesitation can change how a player approaches the game, making them less confident in their abilities and less effective on the field.

How Mental Blocks Impact Rugby Performance

Mental blocks don't just stay in your head—they show up in how you play the game. These invisible barriers can change how you move, think, and work with your team. Mental blocks can hold players back from performing their best and can even affect the team as a whole.

Hesitation During Play

One of the most noticeable ways mental blocks affect performance is through hesitation. Rugby is a sport where every second counts. If you pause too long before making a pass, taking a tackle, or deciding to run with the ball, the opportunity might disappear. Fear of failure and overthinking are often behind this hesitation. Instead of trusting your instincts, you might find yourself second-guessing every move, which slows you down and disrupts the flow of the game. Hesitation can also frustrate teammates who rely on you to make quick decisions and keep the game moving.

Loss of Confidence

Mental blocks like self-doubt can chip away at your confidence, which is a massive part of playing rugby. Confidence gives you the courage to try a new side step, take on a tackler, and hit a ruck. When confidence is low, players may play it safe, avoiding risks or big moments where they could shine. For example, a player who fears failure might avoid kicking for goal during a high-pressure moment, even if they have the skills to slot the kick. Without confidence, it's harder to step up and deliver when it matters most.

Physical Effects of Mental Pressure

Mental blocks can also affect your body. When you're dealing with stress or fear on the field, your muscles can become tense, making it harder to move smoothly and react quickly. You might feel tightness in your shoulders or stiffness in your legs, which can slow you down during sprints or tackles. Mental pressure can also affect your breathing. Shallow, quick breaths can make you tire out faster, leaving you feeling exhausted even if you're in great shape. These physical effects can make rugby feel more difficult than it actually is, all because of what's happening in your mind.

Team Dynamics and Communication

Rugby is a team sport, and mental blocks don't just affect individual players—they can also impact the team as a whole. A player struggling with fear of contact or hesitation might avoid getting involved in key plays, which can force their teammates to cover more ground or take on extra responsibility. This can disrupt the team's strategy and create frustration among players. Communication can also break down if a player is stuck in their own head, making it harder for the team to work together effectively. Mental blocks can create a ripple effect, where one player's struggles affect the performance and morale of the entire team.

Mental blocks are like invisible hurdles that can slow you down or hold you back from reaching your potential. Whether it's fear of failure, overthinking, self-doubt, or fear of contact, these challenges affect how players approach the game, how they feel on the field, and how they connect with their teammates. Recognizing these mental blocks is an important first step for any young rugby player who wants to grow, improve, and enjoy the game. Even though these challenges might seem overwhelming at times, understanding them is key to unlocking your full potential on and off the field.

Mental Blocks & The Rugby Mind

Rugby is as much a mental game as it is a physical one. The brain plays a key role in your performance, helping you think quickly, make decisions, and stay focused under pressure. But sometimes, the brain can get in the way. When mental blocks happen, it feels like your mind is working against you, making it harder to play your best. Understanding how your brain works during these moments can help you recognize why mental blocks happen and how they affect your game.

Scientists have studied mental blocks to understand why skilled players sometimes "freeze" or make mistakes under pressure. Three important parts of the brain play a role in these moments:

the prefrontal cortex, the amygdala, and the motor control systems. Let's look at what each of these does when mental blocks occur.

The Prefrontal Cortex: The Brain's Control Center

The prefrontal cortex, located at the front of your brain, is like your brain's coach. It helps you plan, make decisions, and stay focused on your goals. When you're playing rugby, this part of your brain works hard to help you think through strategies, predict your opponent's moves, and decide whether to run, pass, or kick.

However, the prefrontal cortex can become overwhelmed under pressure. When there's too much stress or anxiety, the prefrontal cortex tries to take control of every little detail. This is called overthinking. For example, instead of instinctively catching a pass, your brain might focus on whether your hands are in the right position or if you're going to drop the ball. This over-control can disrupt your natural skills and make simple actions feel much harder than they are.

The Amygdala: Your Brain's Alarm System

The amygdala is a small part of your brain that acts like an alarm system, keeping you safe from danger. It processes emotions like fear and anxiety and helps your body respond to threats. In rugby, the amygdala is helpful when you need to react quickly to a prop who's charging at you or respond to a knock-on and a change of possession.

However, the amygdala can also cause problems during mental blocks. When the amygdala senses stress, it can trigger the body's fight-or-flight response. This response makes your heart race, your muscles tense up, and your breathing quicken. While this might be helpful in some situations, too much of this response can make it hard to focus and think clearly. For example, if you're worried about missing a tackle, your amygdala might flood your mind with warning signs, making it even harder to stay calm and make the hit.

Motor Control Systems: Turning Thoughts Into Action

Your motor control systems are the parts of your brain and body that turn your thoughts into actions. When you're playing rugby, these systems help you run, tackle, and pass without having to think about every movement. Skilled players rely on muscle memory, which allows their bodies to perform complex actions automatically.

During mental blocks, the connection between your motor control systems and the rest of your brain can break down. This happens because anxiety interferes with muscle memory. Instead of trusting your instincts, you might feel clumsy or unsure of your movements. For example, a rugby player who is usually confident with the ball in hand might knock it on because their brain is trying too hard to control every small movement.

When the prefrontal cortex overthinks, the amygdala overreacts, and the motor systems break down, it's no surprise that performance suffers. These moments can make you feel stuck, like you're not playing the way you know you can.

Mental blocks can affect everything from your confidence to your ability to connect with teammates on the field. They can make you hesitate when you need to act quickly or second-guess yourself in key moments. Recognizing how your brain contributes to these challenges is the first step in overcoming them. Even though mental blocks can feel frustrating, remember that they're a natural part of learning and growing as a player. Even professionals have to overcome mental blocks.

PLAYER PROFILE: JOE MARLER
Navigating Rugby and Mental Health Challenges

Joe Marler, a prop for the Harlequins and a former key player for the England rugby team, is a figure known as much for his powerful presence on the pitch as for his candid openness about mental health struggles. Born on July 7, 1990, in Eastbourne, England, Marler began his rugby journey early, earning a reputation for his strength, skill, and dedication. However, his journey to the top has not been without its challenges, as mental health struggles and mental blocks significantly influenced his career and performance.

Rising to Rugby Stardom

Joe Marler's rugby career blossomed when he joined the Harlequins, quickly establishing himself as one of the premier props in English rugby. His aggressive style of play, scrummaging prowess, and versatility made him a regular for the England national team. Marler contributed to England's Six Nations victories and played a vital role in their runner-up finish at the 2019 Rugby World Cup.

Despite his on-field success, Marler's big personality often masked internal struggles. Known for his humorous antics, including colorful hairstyles and cheeky media comments, Marler projected confidence. However, this exterior concealed deeper issues that began to surface as his career progressed.

Facing Mental Blocks and Depression

Marler's openness about his mental health struggles has been a turning point in rugby's dialogue around emotional well-being. In interviews and his documentary *Big Boys Don't Cry*, Marler has described how mental blocks stemming from anxiety and depression affected his game and personal life. The pressure to perform at the elite level, combined with the physical toll of the sport, left Marler grappling with self-doubt and moments of severe emotional distress .

Marler has acknowledged that his mental health challenges impacted his career in several ways. At times, his depression led to feelings of detachment from the sport he loved. In an interview promoting his book, *Loose Head*, Marler described the difficulty of maintaining focus and motivation, even during pivotal matches. The physical demands of rugby, coupled with the unrelenting need to meet public and professional expectations, compounded his mental struggles. For Marler, moments of self-doubt often arose in high-pressure situations, such as international fixtures, where the stakes were enormous .

Marler also spoke about how societal expectations in rugby culture, which often discourage vulnerability, worsened his struggles. The expectation to appear "tough" created an environment where admitting to mental health issues seemed at odds with being a successful athlete. This internal conflict left Marler battling silently for years before he chose to open up.

Shifting the Conversation

Marler's decision to speak publicly about his mental health has made him a trailblazer in rugby. His candid discussions have resonated with fans and fellow players alike, encouraging more open conversations about mental health within the sport. His documentary and interviews highlight the importance of creating support systems for athletes facing similar challenges.

In *Big Boys Don't Cry*, Marler discusses the personal toll of suppressing emotions and the liberation that comes from addressing them head-on. He hopes his story inspires others in the rugby community to seek help without fear of judgment. The documentary not only sheds light on Marler's journey but also underscores the need for systemic changes in how sports organizations address mental health .

A Legacy Beyond Rugby

Joe Marler's journey illustrates the challenges of balancing elite athletic performance with mental well-being. While he continues to be a dominant force on the pitch, his most significant contributions may be off the field, as he works to normalize mental health discussions in rugby. By sharing his struggles and triumphs, Marler has become a beacon of hope for young players navigating similar challenges.

His story reminds us that even the toughest players can face mental blocks and emotional hurdles. Marler's legacy extends beyond his scrummaging achievements, serving as a testament to the power of vulnerability and resilience. Through his openness, he has not only enriched the sport of rugby but also paved the way for a more compassionate and understanding culture.

Mental blocks can be a powerful barrier to success for young rugby players, affecting performance on and off the field. These mental barriers, whether caused by fear of failure, perfectionism, or self-doubt, have the potential to undermine even the most skilled players. Understanding the impact of mental blocks is the first step toward overcoming them. When left unaddressed, they can lead to hesitation, a lack of confidence, and missed opportunities during critical moments of the game. However, the good news is that mental blocks are not permanent.

The greatest rugby players in the world have faced mental challenges and come out stronger by developing strategies to overcome them. By addressing negative thoughts, building self-awareness, and implementing tools such as mindfulness, positive self-talk, and visualization, young players can unlock their full potential. These tools not only help to overcome mental blocks but also foster resilience and confidence, creating a strong foundation for future challenges.

Rugby is a game of split-second decisions, physical demands, and mental grit. To perform at their best, players must learn to trust their abilities and focus on the present moment. This requires a shift in mindset—from being overly critical of mistakes to seeing them as opportunities for growth. Learning to silence the internal critic and embrace a growth mindset can turn mental blocks into stepping stones toward improvement.

Every player has the capacity to break through their mental blocks. It starts with identifying the specific fears or doubts holding you back, followed by actively working to replace them with empowering thoughts and actions. By committing to small, consistent changes, young rugby players can transform their approach to the game and achieve their goals with greater clarity and determination.

Remember, mental fitness is just as important as physical fitness in rugby. The ability to stay focused, resilient, and adaptable under pressure is what separates good players from great ones. With the right mindset, tools, and support, young players can move beyond their mental barriers, unlocking new levels of performance and enjoyment in the game they love.

As you move through this book, you will learn many different strategies for working through mental blocks. This chapter was designed as the first step, simply identifying the mental blocks. Now is the time to face your mental blocks, embrace the challenges, and step confidently onto the pitch, ready to perform.

3 ACTIVITIES TO HELP YOU OVERCOME MENTAL BARRIERS IN RUGBY

#1 Trigger Tracker

Keep a performance journal to identify patterns that cause mental blocks. After each game or practice, write about moments when you hesitated or underperformed. Detail what was happening, how you felt, and the thoughts running through your mind. Over time, look for recurring triggers and reflect on how you might address them.

Why It Works: Journaling helps players increase self-awareness and recognize the root causes of their mental blocks. By identifying triggers, players can reframe their responses and develop strategies to approach challenging situations with confidence.

#2 Anchor Words for Focus

Select a single word or phrase, like "power," "drive," or "next play," as a focus anchor. Practice using this word during drills or games to regain concentration when distracted. Repeat it silently or under your breath whenever your mind starts to wander or you feel overwhelmed, allowing it to ground you in the present moment. Over time, this habit trains your brain to quickly refocus, helping you perform at your best.

Why It Works: Anchor words are simple mental cues that help players focus on the present moment. They redirect attention away from negative thoughts, providing clarity and motivation.

(#3) Physical Reset Techniques

Practice physical reset actions, like shaking out the arms, clapping hands, or doing a quick sprint after a mistake. Use these as a signal to let go of errors and refocus during games. Pair the action with a deep breath or a positive phrase, such as "reset" or "next play," to reinforce the mental shift. Over time, these physical cues can become automatic, helping you stay composed and mentally sharp, even in high-pressure moments.

Why It Works: Physical movements help interrupt negative thought patterns and provide a mental reset. This keeps players from dwelling on mistakes, allowing them to focus on the next play.

2

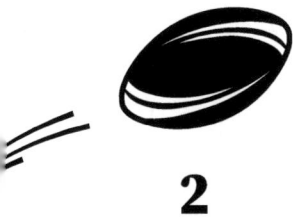

HEAD IN THE GAME:
Emotional Regulation for the Pitch

Rugby is a sport of raw power, precision, and quick decision-making. It requires players to operate in high-stress environments, often with adrenaline pumping and emotions running high. From the thrill of scoring a try to the frustration of a missed tackle, emotional highs and lows are part of the game. However, what separates good players from great ones is the ability to regulate these emotions. Emotional regulation is the skill of managing your feelings so they don't negatively impact your performance or decision-making. For young rugby players, mastering this skill can unlock new levels of focus, resilience, and consistency on the pitch.

What Is Emotional Regulation?

At its core, emotional regulation is about understanding and controlling your emotions rather than letting them control you. It's not about suppressing emotions or pretending they don't exist. Instead, it involves recognizing what you're feeling, assessing the situation, and responding in a way that aligns with your goals. In rugby, this might mean staying calm when the referee makes a controversial call, resetting after a knock-on, or channeling frustration into an intense tackle.

Emotional regulation is closely tied to self-awareness. Recognizing when emotions like anger, fear, or disappointment are bubbling up is the first step toward managing them effectively. Once you're aware of your emotional state, you can address it in a way that keeps you focused and helps your team succeed. This skill doesn't just help on the rugby field; it's also valuable in school, relationships, and other areas of life.

Why Emotional Regulation Matters in Rugby

Rugby is a dynamic and fast-paced game. In the heat of competition, your ability to make smart decisions and execute plays depends on how well you can stay focused and composed. Emotional regulation plays a critical role in several areas of the game:

Decision-Making: Rugby demands quick, calculated decisions, whether it's choosing to pass, kick, carry the ball, or go to ground. When emotions take over, you're more likely to make impulsive decisions that don't benefit your team.

Teamwork: Rugby is a team sport, and communication is key. Emotional outbursts or frustration can strain relationships with teammates and disrupt the team's cohesion.

Resilience: Rugby is physically and mentally demanding. If you let a missed tackle or a tough opponent get under your skin, it can affect your performance for the rest of the game. Emotional regulation helps you bounce back quickly from setbacks.

Consistency: Great rugby players are consistent in their performance. This consistency comes from controlling emotions and maintaining focus, even when things aren't going your way.

By learning to regulate your emotions, you can stay in control during high-pressure situations, recover from mistakes faster, and become a more reliable player for your team.

Emotional Regulation in Action: Great Rugby Players Who Exemplify Control

Some of the greatest rugby players in history have demonstrated exceptional emotional regulation. Their ability to stay composed under pressure and maintain focus during critical moments has set them apart on the field.

One such player is **Richie McCaw**, the legendary New Zealand All Blacks captain. McCaw was renowned for his calm demeanor, even in the most intense matches. Whether it was making crucial decisions in the dying minutes of a game or dealing with physical and verbal challenges from opponents, McCaw's ability to stay composed and lead by example was a key factor in his team's success. His emotional control not only allowed him to perform at his best but also inspired his teammates to do the same.

Another iconic player known for his emotional regulation is **Jonny Wilkinson**, the England fly-half who famously kicked the winning drop goal in the 2003 Rugby World Cup final. Wilkinson's meticulous preparation and ability to block out distractions were legendary. Even under immense pressure, he maintained a laser-like focus that enabled him to execute precision plays. Wilkinson's composure in high-stakes moments made him one of the most reliable players in rugby history.

Siya Kolisi, the captain of the South African Springboks, is another player who demonstrates exceptional emotional regulation. Leading his team to victory in the 2019 Rugby World Cup, Kolisi faced immense pressure as the first Black captain of the Springboks. Despite the weight of expectations, Kolisi's calm leadership and ability to manage his emotions helped unite his team and guide them to glory. His resilience and composure under pressure were a testament to his mental strength.

For young rugby players, these legends serve as wonderful examples of how emotional regulation can elevate your game. They show that staying composed isn't about suppressing passion or intensity; it's about channeling those emotions in a way that benefits your performance and your team.

The Bigger Picture
Emotional regulation isn't just a skill for elite players; it's essential for athletes at every level. Rugby is a sport that demands both physical and mental toughness. By learning to manage your

emotions, you're not only setting yourself up for success on the field but also developing life skills that will serve you well off the pitch.

The journey to mastering emotional regulation is ongoing. Even the best players in the world continue to work on this aspect of their game. As you develop this skill, remember that mistakes and setbacks are part of the process. What matters most is your commitment to improving and your willingness to learn from each experience.

Emotional regulation is a game-changer for young rugby players. It's the foundation for resilience, focus, and consistent performance. By looking to role models like Richie McCaw, Jonny Wilkinson, and Siya Kolisi, you can see what's possible when you stay composed under pressure. Whether you're leading your team, bouncing back from a poor pass, or preparing for a critical match, emotional regulation will help you rise to the challenge and make your mark on the game.

The Science Behind Emotional Regulation

Emotional regulation plays a crucial role in athletic performance, particularly in high-intensity sports like rugby. The science behind emotional regulation highlights the interplay between the brain's structure, stress responses, and cognitive control, all of which are necessary for young athletes learning to manage their emotions on and off the field.

The Role of the Prefrontal Cortex in Emotional Regulation
The prefrontal cortex (PFC) is the brain's command center for decision-making, focus, and self-regulation. It works to suppress impulsive reactions and align behaviors with long-term goals, like maintaining composure and executing plays under pressure. For young rugby players, a well-functioning PFC supports their ability to think strategically and remain composed, even when emotions are heightened by the physical and competitive nature of the game.

The Brain's Stress Response and Emotional Regulation

Stress is an inevitable aspect of rugby, whether it stems from physical challenges, competitive tension, or setbacks during a game. When players encounter stress, the body releases cortisol, the primary stress hormone. In small doses, cortisol can enhance alertness and reaction times, which is beneficial for rugby performance. However, chronic or poorly managed stress leads to an overactivation of cortisol, negatively impacting thinking and emotional regulation.

Strong emotional regulation minimizes these effects by reducing stress responses. Through shifting thinking, or changing the interpretation of a situation—players can maintain a sense of control. For example, reframing a referee's unfavorable decision as a challenge rather than an injustice can help maintain focus and energy for the next play.

The Connection Between Emotion and Performance

Effective emotional regulation ensures that emotional intensity remains within an optimal range. This range, often referred to as the "zone of optimal functioning," is where players can harness their energy and focus without being overwhelmed by negative emotions. For young rugby players, learning to regulate emotions grows resilience, allowing them to bounce back from mistakes and maintain their confidence throughout the game.

By recognizing how the brain manages emotions and adapts to stress, players can better prepare themselves to thrive under the intense demands of rugby. Through consistent practice and awareness, they can develop the mental fitness needed to perform at their best, regardless of the challenges they face on the pitch.

PLAYER PROFILE: DAN CARTER
Emotional Mastery

Dan Carter, one of the greatest rugby players of all time, is celebrated not only for his exceptional skills but also for his unwavering emotional control under pressure. The former All Blacks fly-half has spoken extensively about how his ability to regulate emotions became a cornerstone of his success, allowing him to thrive in high-stakes situations. For rugby players seeking to enhance their performance, Carter's story is a valuable lesson in mastering emotional regulation.

The Challenge of Pressure

Throughout his illustrious career, Carter faced immense expectations, particularly in the 2015 Rugby World Cup, where the All Blacks aimed to shed their "chokers" label. Despite being under the global spotlight, Carter consistently delivered match-winning performances, culminating in a decisive role during the final against Australia. His ability to remain composed and focused during such critical moments was no accident; it was the result of deliberate mental preparation.

Carter attributes his success under pressure to focusing on the process rather than the outcome. As he explained in a Forbes interview, shifting attention from external pressures—such as winning a match or the expectations of fans—allowed him to remain calm and perform his role effectively. By concentrating on tasks like perfecting his kicking technique or executing accurate passes, Carter minimized distractions and maintained clarity even during the most intense moments.

The Power of Emotional Regulation

Emotional regulation, or the ability to manage one's emotional responses, was a skill Carter honed through experience and reflection. Early in his career, he struggled with nerves and self-doubt, particularly during critical matches. However, over time, he developed strategies to keep his emotions in check. One of his key techniques was deep breathing, a practice that helped him lower his heart rate and stay grounded during pressure-packed moments.

Another critical aspect of Carter's emotional control was his mindset. He embraced a "process-oriented" approach, which helped him handle stress more effectively. By focusing on what he could control—like preparation, effort, and execution—he freed himself from the paralyzing fear of failure. This approach not only improved his performance but also allowed him to enjoy the game, even in the most challenging scenarios.

Lessons for Rugby Players

Dan Carter's journey offers practical lessons in emotional regulation. First, it highlights the importance of preparation. Carter's detailed pre-game routines, including visualization and practicing under simulated pressure, ensured he felt confident and ready. Second, his focus on the process underscores the value of concentrating on the present moment rather than worrying about the outcome.

Finally, Carter's story demonstrates the transformative power of self-awareness. By recognizing his emotional triggers and addressing them with actionable strategies, Carter turned potential weaknesses into strengths. Young players can adopt similar practices, such as setting achievable goals, staying mindful of their breathing, and reframing challenges as opportunities.

Dan Carter's legacy as a rugby legend extends beyond his physical skills; his mastery of emotional control sets him apart as a player who could perform when it mattered most. By learning from his methods and mindset, young athletes can develop the mental resilience needed to excel in rugby and beyond.

Conclusion: Harnessing Emotional Regulation for Rugby Success

Emotional regulation is more than a mental skill; it is a cornerstone of athletic success, particularly in a high-stakes sport like rugby. The ability to stay composed and make clear, rational decisions under pressure separates good players from great ones. It empowers athletes to recover from mistakes, adapt to challenging situations, and maintain consistency on the field. For aspiring rugby players, mastering this skill is as important as developing physical strength or honing technical abilities.

The stories of legends like Dan Carter, Richie McCaw, and Siya Kolisi illuminate the power of emotional control. Their ability to stay composed in the face of adversity and to lead with focus and clarity is a testament to the transformative impact of emotional regulation. These players showed that controlling emotions doesn't mean suppressing passion—it means channeling it effectively.

But, emotional regulation begins with self-awareness. Recognizing when frustration, anxiety, or fear is building is the first step toward managing these emotions. Developing actionable strategies, like deep breathing, visualization, and process-focused thinking, gives athletes the tools to navigate high-pressure moments. These practices not only enhance performance but also build resilience, helping players bounce back stronger from setbacks.

Emotional regulation is a skill that transcends the rugby field. It contributes to better communication with teammates, stronger leadership, and a balanced perspective in both sports and life. As rugby players strive to develop this skill, they should remember that mastery doesn't happen overnight. It requires patience, practice, and a willingness to learn from mistakes.

Ultimately, emotional regulation is about unlocking your potential and helping your team succeed. Whether you're preparing for a critical match, leading by example, or overcoming a tough play, staying composed under pressure will set you apart. By embracing the lessons from rugby's greats and committing to personal growth, athletes can transform emotional regulation into a competitive advantage that elevates their game and character alike.

3 ACTIVITIES TO HELP YOU DEVELOP YOUR EMOTIONAL REGULATION

#1 Box Breathing

Practice a technique called "box breathing." Sit in a comfortable position, inhale deeply for four counts, hold your breath for four counts, exhale for four counts, and hold again for four counts. Repeat this cycle for 2-3 minutes, focusing on the rhythm of your breath and the sensation of air filling your lungs. Use this exercise before games, during breaks, or after a stressful play to reset your emotional state.

Why It Works: Deep breathing activates the parasympathetic nervous system, which helps calm the body's stress response. By slowing your breathing, you lower your heart rate and reduce cortisol levels, the stress hormone. This shift enables clearer thinking and better decision-making under pressure. It also reinforces the habit of staying present and focused, which is essential for performing well in dynamic situations.

#2 Emotional Journaling

After games or practice, spend 5-10 minutes writing about your emotional experiences. Note situations that triggered strong emotions, how you responded, and what you learned. End the session by identifying one thing you did well and one area for improvement.

Why It Works: Journaling builds self-awareness, a key component of emotional regulation. Reflecting on emotional triggers helps you understand patterns in your behavior and equips you to manage similar situations in the future. This process turns emotional setbacks into growth opportunities, allowing you to approach challenges with a clearer and more resilient mindset.

(#3) Anchor Phrases

Identify a calming phrase, such as "Stay in control" or "One play at a time." Practice repeating this phrase to yourself during training sessions when emotions start to rise, and use it during games to refocus your mind after a mistake or high-pressure moment. Pair the phrase with a deep breath to reinforce its calming effect.

Why It Works: Anchor phrases act as mental cues that interrupt emotional escalation. By focusing on a pre-chosen phrase, you create a moment of pause that prevents reactive behavior. Over time, this technique becomes an automatic response to stress, helping you remain composed and in control during critical moments.

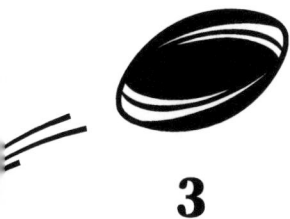

3

MENTAL MAUL:
Visualizing Victory on the Rugby Field

Have you ever imagined yourself scoring the match-winning try just as the final whistle blows or sidestepping past multiple defenders on a highlight run? If you have, then you've already started using a technique called visualization. Visualization, also known as mental imagery, is the practice of creating detailed pictures in your mind of how you want to perform on the field. Many elite rugby players use this skill to prepare mentally for their games, improve their abilities, and build confidence. For aspiring rugby players, learning how to use visualization can be a game-changer, helping you see yourself as a stronger, faster, and more composed player before you even step onto the pitch.

You might wonder, "How can simply imagining myself playing rugby make me better at it?" It sounds almost too good to be true, but visualization works because your brain doesn't fully know the difference between real and imagined experiences. When you visualize yourself performing a rugby skill—like passing accurately, tackling effectively, or scoring a try—your brain sends signals to your muscles, even though you're not physically moving. These mental signals create a "muscle memory" blueprint, preparing your body to follow through with these actions in a real game. Visualization is like a mental workout for your brain, strengthening your ability to make plays and decisions exactly how you've imagined.

What Is Visualization?

Visualization is much more than daydreaming or simply hoping things will go well in a game. It's a focused, intentional technique where you imagine each detail of what you want to accomplish on the field. When you visualize, you should try to include every part of the experience: the feel of the rugby ball in your hands, the sight of the opposition's defensive line, the sound of the crowd cheering, and even the emotions you feel as you execute the play. By mentally picturing these details, you're creating a virtual practice session in your mind, preparing your brain and body to react confidently and effectively when it's game time.

How Does It Help Rugby Players?

Visualization can be helpful for a variety of situations on the rugby field. For instance, you can use it before a game to mentally rehearse how you'll handle key moments, such as kicking a conversion under pressure or executing a perfect line-out. You can also use it during training to prepare for specific skills, like mastering your tackling technique or improving your passing accuracy. Some players even use visualization to picture themselves overcoming challenges, like bouncing back after a missed tackle or regaining focus after a turnover. This technique helps you not only improve physically but also build mental strength, making you a more resilient and focused player.

Building Confidence

One reason visualization is so powerful is that it can actually improve your confidence. When you see yourself succeeding in your mind, your brain starts to believe that success is possible.

Imagine you're nervous about an upcoming match. You can use visualization to picture yourself playing well, making smart decisions, and scoring tries. By practicing these images in your mind, you're showing yourself that you're capable of achieving these things, which helps reduce nerves and boost your confidence when the match begins. Over time, these positive mental images help you trust your abilities more and push through tough situations on the field.

Improving Focus

Another important benefit of visualization is that it improves focus. Rugby is a fast-paced sport with plenty of distractions, from the opposing team's strategies to the noise of the crowd. Visualization helps you practice concentrating on your goals, like keeping your eyes on the ball or staying aware of your teammates' positions. By mentally rehearsing how you want to perform, you train your brain to stay focused on what's important, even when distractions are present. This skill makes it easier to block out noise, stay calm under pressure, and keep your attention on the play in front of you.

Sharpening Skills

In addition to building confidence and improving focus, visualization can also help sharpen your skills. When you visualize yourself practicing a skill, like a perfect pass or packing down a strong scrum, your brain activates the same pathways it would if you were physically practicing the skill. This is called "mental rehearsal," and it's been shown to improve coordination, reaction time, and decision-making. Let's say you're working on your sidestepping technique. By visualizing yourself evading defenders with quick, precise movements, you can practice the actions mentally, making it easier to execute them physically when you're actually on the pitch. It's like getting extra practice without even picking up the ball.

Preparing for Pressure Situations

Visualization also prepares you for high-pressure situations in rugby. Let's say it's the final minutes of a close game, and you have a penalty kick to win the match. By mentally rehearsing this situation, you can prepare yourself to stay calm and focused under pressure. Visualization helps you control your nerves by showing you exactly how you want to react at that moment, building a sense of familiarity that makes it easier to perform well when the pressure is on. Practicing these pressure situations in your mind can make them feel less intimidating when they happen in real life.

In summary, visualization is an incredibly useful tool for young rugby players. It helps build confidence by showing you that success is possible, improves focus by training your brain to stay on task, and sharpens your skills through mental practice. Whether you're a fly-half aiming for precise passes or a front rower working on your scrummaging technique, visualization gives you an edge that goes beyond physical training. By regularly practicing this technique, you'll be able to step onto the pitch feeling prepared, focused, and ready to perform.

The Science Behind Visualization

When rugby players practice visualization, their brains engage in a powerful process that enhances performance on the field. Visualization activates neural pathways in the brain that mimic those used during physical movement. Even though the body remains still, the brain signals muscles to prepare for specific actions, creating a mental blueprint of the skills needed to perform. For example, picturing yourself executing a perfect spin pass or breaking through a tackle trains your brain to coordinate these movements more effectively during a game.

This mental rehearsal strengthens the brain-muscle connection, improving coordination, reaction time, and decision-making. Key brain regions become involved during visualization, such as the motor cortex, which plans movements, and the prefrontal cortex, responsible for strategy and decision-making. Meanwhile, the limbic system, which manages emotions, helps players regulate feelings of anxiety or excitement. By repeatedly visualizing successful actions, rugby players build confidence and develop the mental readiness to handle high-pressure situations.

In addition, visualization triggers the brain's reward system, releasing dopamine—a neurotransmitter linked to motivation and focus. These positive effects reduce performance anxiety and enhance self-belief. The brain begins to associate the imagined success with real outcomes, making it easier to execute skills under stress.

For rugby players, visualization isn't just a mental exercise—it's a tool that builds mental toughness, sharpens focus, and improves physical execution. By consistently practicing this technique, aspiring athletes can enhance their preparation, adapt to challenges, and boost their overall performance on the field.

PLAYER PROFILE: PORTIA WOODMAN
Victorious with Visualization

Portia Woodman, a trailblazing figure in women's rugby, has earned a reputation as one of the sport's most electrifying players. Born in Kaikohe, New Zealand, in 1991, Woodman initially made her mark as a sprinter before transitioning to rugby. Her remarkable speed, agility, and finishing ability quickly catapulted her to international stardom.

Woodman began her rugby career with the New Zealand Women's Sevens team in 2013, where she demonstrated her unmatched talent on the field. She was instrumental in New Zealand's gold-medal victory at the 2020 Tokyo Olympics and has been a key player in numerous World Rugby Sevens Series championships. Equally fierce in the 15-a-side game, Woodman has excelled as a winger for the Black Ferns, helping them secure the Rugby World Cup in 2017. Her accomplishments include being named World Rugby Women's Player of the Year in 2015 and becoming one of the highest try-scorers in rugby history.

Central to Woodman's success is her commitment to mental preparation, particularly her use of visualization techniques. In interviews, Woodman has shared how visualization helps her prepare for high-pressure moments on the field. Before matches, she mentally rehearses scenarios such as breaking through defensive lines, making precise passes, or scoring decisive tries. She imagines the sights, sounds, and emotions of game day to create a vivid mental simulation. This practice not only boosts her confidence but also sharpens her focus, ensuring she is mentally and physically ready for pivotal moments.

Woodman has also spoken about the spiritual aspect of her preparation, blending visualization with her values and sense of purpose. This holistic approach reinforces her resilience and helps her stay grounded amidst the pressures of elite competition. Whether envisioning success on the field or reflecting on her performances, visualization remains a cornerstone of her routine.

Portia Woodman's career is a testament to the power of mental preparation paired with exceptional athletic ability. Her dedication to visualization has enabled her to thrive on the world stage, making her a role model for aspiring rugby players and an icon in women's sports.

Conclusion: Using Visualization in Preparation

Visualization is more than just imagining success; it's a transformative tool that bridges the gap between mental preparation and physical execution. For rugby players, mastering this mental skill can make the difference between a good and exceptional performance. By painting vivid mental pictures of success, athletes create a mental map for their brains to follow, building confidence, sharpening focus, and preparing for high-pressure scenarios.

The impact of visualization extends beyond the individual skills practiced. It fosters resilience, enabling players to bounce back from setbacks and stay composed under pressure. Whether it's a winger anticipating the perfect sidestep or a fly-half rehearsing a game-winning drop goal, visualization instills belief in one's abilities and readiness to tackle challenges head-on.

For rugby players, incorporating visualization into their routine sets the stage for a balanced approach to rugby—one that values mental fitness as much as physical preparation. Just as hours on the training pitch refine skills, consistent mental rehearsal enhances precision, reaction time, and decision-making during games. With visualization, players can take the lessons learned in practice and see themselves executing flawlessly in real match situations.

Portia Woodman's remarkable journey exemplifies how visualization can elevate performance. Her use of mental imagery to rehearse scenarios, sharpen focus, and stay connected to her values emphasizes the profound impact of visualization. It's a practice that not only contributes to winning on the field but also builds the character and confidence required to succeed in life beyond rugby.

As you step onto the rugby field, remember the power of visualization. Envision yourself confidently making committed tackles, executing perfect passes, or scoring game-changing tries. With regular practice, you'll see its effects not just on the scoreboard but in how you approach every challenge. Visualization isn't just about winning games—it's about becoming the best version of yourself, both on and off the pitch.

3 ACTIVITIES TO HELP YOU WITH VISUALIZATION & MENTAL IMAGERY

#1 Game-Day Mental Rehearsal

Before a match, sit in a quiet space and spend 10-15 minutes mentally walking through the game. Imagine the moments you'll face on the field—how you'll catch the ball, make a pass, or execute a tackle. Include vivid sensory details: the feel of the ball, the sounds of the crowd, and the movements of your teammates and opponents. Picture yourself handling pressure situations, like scoring a try or making a crucial defensive play.

Why It Works: Mental rehearsal helps your brain create a neural blueprint of the actions you want to execute. By imagining specific scenarios, you prepare yourself to react confidently and effectively in real-game situations. The vivid sensory details trick your brain into believing the practice is real, which builds muscle memory, sharpens decision-making, and reduces anxiety when similar situations arise on the field.

#2 Highlight Reel Visualization

Create a mental "highlight reel" of your best plays from past games or training sessions. Close your eyes and replay these moments, focusing on what made them successful—your positioning, timing, or technique. Afterward, visualize performing similar skills in an upcoming match. Add new scenarios where you see yourself improving or mastering a skill you've been practicing.

Why It Works: Reflecting on past successes boosts confidence and reinforces positive self-belief. Revisiting these moments helps you focus on your strengths and reminds you that you're capable of performing well under pressure. By combining past highlights with new goals, you prime your mind for future success, blending familiarity with growth.

(#3) Skill-Specific Visualization

Choose a rugby skill you want to improve, such as sidestepping, tackling, or kicking. Visualize yourself performing the skill perfectly in slow motion, focusing on each detail: your stance, body movement, and execution. Gradually increase the pace of your visualization until it matches the game speed. Repeat this daily.

Why It Works: Skill-specific visualization engages the same neural pathways as physical practice. This mental rehearsal strengthens your brain's ability to coordinate precise movements, making it easier to replicate them on the field. Slow-motion visualization allows you to focus on technique, while game-speed visualization reinforces muscle memory for real-time execution.

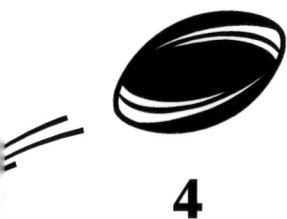

4

THROUGH THE PHASES:
Elevating Your Game with a Growth Mindset

In rugby, physical strength, speed, and tactical training are undeniably important, but the way you think about your abilities—especially your capacity to grow and improve—can make the biggest difference. Enter the growth mindset: a powerful mental approach that can help players overcome challenges, continuously develop their skills, and unlock their full potential on and off the pitch.

A growth mindset is the belief that talents, skills, and intelligence can be developed through effort, effective strategies, and feedback from others. It's the opposite of a fixed mindset, where individuals believe their abilities are static and unchangeable. For rugby players, adopting a growth mindset can mean the difference between plateauing after early success and continuously striving to be better, improving skills and abilities every game. By believing in their potential to improve, young athletes can embrace challenges, recover from setbacks, and learn from their mistakes.

What is a Growth Mindset?

Psychologist Carol Dweck introduced the terms "growth mindset" and "fixed mindset" to describe how people perceive their abilities. According to Dweck, individuals with a growth mindset view setbacks and obstacles as opportunities to grow, while those with a fixed mindset see them as proof of their limitations. For aspiring rugby players, having a growth mindset means believing that every skill — whether it's tackling, passing, rucking, or decision-making under pressure — can be improved with practice and dedication.

In rugby, a fixed mindset might show up as thoughts like, "I'm just not fast enough to play on the wing" or "I'm not good at kicking." This mindset can lead players to avoid challenging situations, fearing failure and criticism. On the other hand, a player with a growth mindset would see these as opportunities for improvement. Instead of thinking, "I'm bad at this," they might say, "I'm not good at this yet, but with effort and practice, I can get better."

Why a Growth Mindset Matters for Rugby Players

A growth mindset doesn't just shape how you approach challenges; it transforms how you respond to every part of the game. Rugby is a sport that demands resilience, adaptability, and continuous improvement. Players will face moments of defeat, make mistakes on the field, and encounter opponents who seem unbeatable. The difference between players who grow and those who don't often comes down to mindset. With a growth mindset, mistakes become opportunities to learn, not reasons to give up.

Consider some of the world's most successful rugby players. Many of them have faced injuries, tough losses, or personal struggles along their journey. What set them apart was their belief in their ability to improve and adapt. For young players, developing a growth mindset means building the resilience to keep pushing forward, even when progress feels slow. It's about embracing the process of improvement and focusing on long-term growth rather than immediate results.

Benefits of a Growth Mindset in Rugby

Improved Resilience

One of the most significant advantages of a growth mindset

is improved resilience. Rugby is a physically and mentally demanding sport, requiring players to stay focused and bounce back quickly from setbacks. A growth mindset encourages players to view mistakes and losses as part of the learning process rather than reasons to feel discouraged. This perspective helps them return stronger and tackle challenges head-on.

Imagine a player who struggles with lineout throws during a match. A fixed mindset might lead him to think, "I'll never get this right," causing him to lose confidence and avoid practicing. However, with a growth mindset, he might say, "This is an area I can improve," leading to dedicated practice sessions and constructive feedback from his coach. Over time, this attitude not only improves his throwing accuracy but also strengthens his ability to handle pressure and adversity.

Increased Confidence and Motivation
When players believe they can improve through effort, they naturally feel more confident in their abilities. This confidence isn't based on being perfect but on the belief that progress is always possible. Rugby players with a growth mindset are more likely to approach tough training sessions with enthusiasm, stay motivated during demanding drills, and maintain confidence even during challenging matches.

This mindset also fosters a love for learning and growth. Players set realistic goals, celebrate incremental progress, and understand that every small improvement contributes to their overall development. For example, a player working on their tackling technique might focus on mastering proper positioning and timing. Each successful tackle boosts their confidence and fuels their motivation to keep improving.

Better Performance
Over time, a growth mindset leads to better performance on the field. Players with this mindset understand that excellence in rugby isn't achieved overnight; it's the result of consistent effort and perseverance. They embrace hard work and view feedback as a tool for growth rather than criticism.

In practical terms, this might involve spending extra time practicing kicks after training, seeking advice from coaches, or analyzing game footage to identify areas for improvement. Players with a growth mindset are also more willing to step out of their comfort zones, whether it's trying new techniques, taking on leadership roles, or competing against stronger opponents.

Strengthened Team Dynamics

Rugby is a team sport, and players with a growth mindset contribute positively to team dynamics. This mindset fosters a supportive and collaborative environment where teammates encourage one another and work together to improve. Instead of focusing solely on individual performance, players with a growth mindset recognize the importance of collective growth and success, and they push one another to get better.

For instance, if a teammate drops a crucial pass, a player with a growth mindset might offer constructive feedback or words of encouragement rather than expressing frustration. They understand that everyone has room to grow and that fostering a positive team culture benefits the entire squad.

How to Develop a Growth Mindset

Developing a growth mindset takes time and effort, but the rewards are well worth it. Here are some steps to help young rugby players embrace this powerful approach:

Shift Your Language: Pay attention to the way you talk to yourself. Replace fixed-mindset phrases like, "I can't do this" with growth-oriented statements like, "I can't do this yet, but I'm working on it." This simple change reinforces the belief that improvement is possible.

Embrace Challenges: Instead of avoiding difficult situations, view them as opportunities to grow. Whether it's playing against a stronger team or learning a new position, stepping out of your comfort zone helps you develop new skills and build resilience.

Seek Feedback: Constructive feedback from coaches, teammates, and mentors is a valuable tool for growth. Instead of feeling discouraged by criticism, use it as a guide for areas where you can improve.

Celebrate Effort and Progress: Recognize and celebrate the effort you put into improving, even if the results aren't immediate. Success in rugby is often about consistent effort over time, so focus on the journey rather than just the outcomes.

Set Goals: Break your development into achievable goals, such as improving your passing accuracy or increasing your fitness level. Track your progress and adjust your goals as you grow.

Adopting a growth mindset is a game-changer for rugby players. It teaches you to see challenges as opportunities, embrace mistakes as learning experiences, and strive for continuous improvement. Your potential isn't fixed; it's something you can develop with every training session, match, and moment of reflection. By believing in your ability to grow, you're setting yourself up not only for success on the rugby field but also for resilience and adaptability in life. As you embark on your rugby journey, remember: growth is a process, and every step forward counts.

The Science Behind a Growth Mindset

The brain science behind a growth mindset is deeply connected to neuroplasticity—the brain's extraordinary ability to reorganize itself and create new neural connections through practice and experience. This adaptability means that with consistent effort, rugby players can enhance their skills, learn new techniques, and ultimately improve their performance on the field. Embracing a growth mindset fuels this process, as players who believe in their capacity to grow are more likely to put in the hard work required for improvement.

When a player practices a rugby-specific skill, such as tackling, kicking, or passing, neurons in their brain form and strengthen pathways associated with that skill. This focused practice solidifies neural connections, making movements feel more automatic over time. A growth mindset encourages players to push through challenges, understanding that their effort directly contributes to this brain development.

On the other hand, a fixed mindset can impede progress. Players who view their abilities as unchangeable may shy away from difficult drills or give up after mistakes, hindering the brain's ability to adapt and grow. This self-limiting belief disrupts the natural process of forming and reinforcing neural pathways.

In addition, adopting a growth mindset triggers the release of dopamine, a neurotransmitter linked to motivation and reward. Celebrating small victories or noticing progress can elevate dopamine levels, creating a positive feedback loop that reinforces persistence and enjoyment in learning. By understanding the science behind neuroplasticity and growth mindset, young rugby players can embrace challenges, persist through setbacks, and unlock their full potential both on and off the pitch.

PLAYER PROFILE: SIYA KOLISI
A Journey of Resilience and Growth Mindset

Siya Kolisi, the first black captain of South Africa's national rugby team, is a beacon of hope, resilience, and determination. His journey from the impoverished township of Zwide to lifting the Webb Ellis Cup as a World Cup-winning captain embodies the essence of a growth mindset—the belief that abilities can be developed through hard work, perseverance, and embracing challenges.

Humble Beginnings

Kolisi was born on June 16, 1991, in Zwide, a township near Port Elizabeth. Life in Zwide was far from easy. Growing up in poverty, Kolisi often went to bed hungry and wore clothes passed down from others. His mother passed away when he was just 15, leaving his grandmother to raise him. Despite these challenges, young Siya found solace and purpose in rugby, a sport that would eventually change his life.

Kolisi's talent on the field was evident from an early age. Spotted by scouts while playing in a township tournament, he earned a scholarship to Grey High School, one of South Africa's most prestigious rugby institutions. The transition was not easy. Kolisi had to adapt to a new environment, culture, and expectations. However, his relentless determination and willingness to learn saw him flourish both academically and athletically.

Rising Through the Ranks

After excelling in schoolboy rugby, Kolisi joined the Western Province Rugby Academy. His hard work and commitment quickly paid off, as he debuted for the Stormers in Super Rugby in 2012. From there, his career trajectory continued to rise. In 2013, he made his international debut for the Springboks against Scotland. Kolisi's ability to remain grounded and focused, even when faced with setbacks like injuries or intense competition, highlighted his growth mindset.

Kolisi's leadership qualities were unmistakable. In 2018, he was named the captain of the Springboks, becoming the first black player in South Africa's history to hold this position. This appointment was not just a personal achievement but a significant moment for a nation still grappling with its apartheid legacy.

Embracing a Growth Mindset

Throughout his career, Kolisi has consistently demonstrated the principles of a growth mindset. He acknowledges that setbacks and challenges are inevitable but views them as opportunities to learn and grow. "You can't control what happens to you, but you can control how you respond to it," Kolisi often says. This philosophy has shaped his approach to rugby and life.

Kolisi's leadership was tested during the 2019 Rugby World Cup. South Africa's journey to the tournament was filled with challenges, including injuries and doubts about their form. As captain, Kolisi inspired his team with his unwavering belief in preparation, teamwork, and resilience. His ability to build unity within a diverse squad—composed of players from varying backgrounds—was pivotal to their success.

When the Springboks triumphed over England in the final, Kolisi's emotional post-match speech resonated globally. He spoke of gratitude, teamwork, and the importance of giving back to the community. The image of Kolisi lifting the trophy became a symbol of hope and progress for South Africa.

Beyond Rugby

Kolisi's growth mindset extends beyond the rugby field. In 2020, he and his wife Rachel founded the Kolisi Foundation, focusing on community development, education, and addressing social inequalities. Through the foundation, Kolisi has worked tirelessly to uplift underserved communities, providing resources and opportunities for those in need.

Despite his fame and success, Kolisi remains humble and committed to self-improvement. He has spoken openly about the importance of mental health, learning from mistakes, and the role of faith in his life. His resilience and willingness to embrace vulnerability make him a relatable and inspiring figure.

Legacy and Impact

Siya Kolisi's story is more than just a tale of sporting success; it's a narrative of overcoming adversity and redefining leadership. By adopting a growth mindset, Kolisi has shown that greatness isn't confined to natural talent but is grown through hard work, adaptability, and an unwavering belief in oneself.

From the dusty fields of Zwide to the grand stages of international rugby, Kolisi's journey is a testament to the power of resilience and a growth-oriented approach. He continues to inspire millions, proving that no matter where you come from, with determination and the right mindset, you can achieve greatness.

Conclusion: Unlocking Your Rugby Potential with a Growth Mindset

As you progress through your rugby journey, one truth stands out: your mindset shapes your path as much as your physical skills do. Adopting a growth mindset is about recognizing that your abilities are not fixed but can be developed through effort, persistence, and a willingness to learn. This mindset doesn't just impact your performance on the field—it transforms how you approach challenges, setbacks, and opportunities in every aspect of life.

Rugby is a demanding sport that requires grit, adaptability, and teamwork. You'll face moments of triumph and moments of frustration, but with a growth mindset, you'll see every experience as a chance to improve. Instead of being discouraged by a missed tackle or a lost game, you'll find ways to learn, grow, and come back stronger.

A growth mindset empowers you to focus on the process rather than just the results. It's about celebrating small victories— improved passing accuracy, better endurance, or sharper decision-making under pressure—because every step forward contributes to your overall development. When you view challenges as opportunities and failures as learning experiences, you unlock a resilience that propels you toward your full potential.

Remember, growth isn't a straight line. There will be ups and downs, but each moment presents a choice: to give up or to push forward. Players like Siya Kolisi, who faced significant challenges yet rose to the pinnacle of rugby, demonstrate that a belief in growth, combined with relentless effort, can lead to extraordinary achievements.

You have the tools to elevate your game and the power to shape your future. By adopting a growth mindset, you'll not only improve your skills but also inspire those around you. Rugby is a team sport, and when you embrace growth, you contribute to the collective success of your squad. You foster an environment where everyone strives to be better and supports one another along the way.

So, as you lace up your boots, step onto the field, and tackle the next challenge, remember this: your potential is limitless. Growth is a journey, not a destination. Trust in your ability to improve, seek feedback, embrace challenges, and stay committed to the process. The mental skills you develop in rugby will serve you far beyond the game, equipping you with the resilience, confidence, and determination to thrive in all areas of life.

3 ACTIVITIES TO HELP YOU WITH DEVELOPING A GROWTH MINDSET

#1 Embrace the "Not Yet" Mindset

When faced with a challenge—like struggling to perfect a tackle, kick a drop goal, hit a lineout throw, or master a complex play—replace negative thoughts like "I'll never get this" with "I haven't mastered this yet." Say this phrase out loud or write it down when practicing challenging skills to create a habit of optimistic thinking.

Why It Works: The "not yet" mindset shifts focus from immediate results to the ongoing process of learning. By reframing failure as temporary, players reduce self-doubt and build resilience. This approach aligns with the principles of neuroplasticity, as consistent effort strengthens neural pathways over time, ultimately improving performance.

#2 Growth Partner System

Pair up with a teammate to act as each other's accountability and growth partner. Set personal goals and share them with your partner, who will provide support, encouragement, and constructive feedback. Celebrate each other's successes and brainstorm solutions when setbacks arise.

Why It Works: Having a growth partner creates a positive feedback loop where players motivate each other to stay focused and improve. It fosters a culture of collaboration and builds a supportive environment, helping players internalize the belief that growth is both an individual and team pursuit.

(#3) Challenge-of-the-Week

Choose one area of rugby to focus on for the week, such as improving lineout throws or defensive positioning. Set specific, measurable goals (e.g., "Execute five perfect throws during drills today") and ask a coach or teammate for feedback. At the end of the week, assess your progress and set a new challenge.

Why It Works: Focusing on one challenge at a time helps players break their development into manageable steps. This method encourages deliberate practice and ensures steady progress without overwhelming them. Feedback from others provides valuable insights, reinforcing that improvement is a collaborative and continuous process.

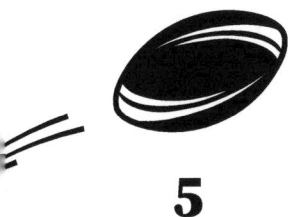

5

TACKLING TOUGH TIMES:
Building Resilience On and Off the Pitch

In the physically demanding and mentally challenging world of rugby, resilience and grit are two qualities that separate good players from great ones. These traits not only help players thrive on the field but also carry over into their personal lives, equipping them to face adversity and achieve long-term goals.

What is Resilience?

Resilience is the ability to recover quickly from setbacks, adapt to adversity, and keep moving forward. In rugby, setbacks come in many forms: a missed tackle, a lost game, or even an injury. Resilient players don't dwell on their mistakes or let negative experiences define them. Instead, they focus on learning from these challenges and improving their performance.

Resilience also involves emotional regulation, enabling players to maintain composure in high-pressure situations. A resilient rugby player can stay calm under the intense scrutiny of a packed sideline, make rational decisions during chaotic matches, and bounce back emotionally after a tough loss.

What is Grit?

Grit, on the other hand, is the combination of passion and perseverance toward long-term goals. In rugby, this means staying committed to consistent improvement, whether it's building specific skills, increasing fitness levels, or mastering the mental aspects of the game. Gritty players are driven by their love for the sport and their determination to achieve their full potential, no matter how long or difficult the journey.

Grit often shows up as relentless effort, even when progress is slow or obstacles seem insurmountable. A gritty rugby player will show up to every practice, push through fatigue, and maintain focus on their goals despite obstacles or distractions.

The Difference Between Resilience and Grit

While resilience and grit are closely related, they serve different purposes. Resilience is reactive, enabling players to recover from setbacks and adapt to challenges. Grit is proactive, focusing on sustained effort and dedication over the long term. In rugby, resilience might help a player shake off a mistake during a game and refocus on the next play, while grit ensures they keep training hard to improve their skills in the weeks and months ahead.

Another key distinction lies in their emotional and mental focus. Resilience often involves managing immediate emotions, such as frustration or disappointment, and transforming them into productive energy. For instance, a resilient player might channel the sting of a missed opportunity into renewed determination for the remainder of the game. Grit, however, requires maintaining motivation over time, even when progress feels slow or when the initial excitement for a goal has faded. It is the ability to keep the bigger picture in mind and remain steadfast in pursuit of improvement.

Handling Pressure and Overcoming Injuries and Setbacks

Rugby is a high-pressure sport where split-second decisions can make or break a game. Resilient players manage their emotions effectively, keeping a clear head when executing plays or making critical tackles. Grit ensures that players stay committed to their preparation, building the confidence needed to perform under pressure.

Injuries are an unfortunate reality of rugby. Resilience helps players maintain a positive outlook during rehabilitation, while grit motivates them to stick with their recovery routines and return to the field stronger than before. Together, these qualities prevent setbacks from derailing a player's career.

Developing Skills and Fostering Team Cohesion

Rugby demands a wide range of skills, from technical abilities like passing and tackling to strategic thinking and teamwork. Grit drives players to continually refine these skills, often through repetitive practice and learning from failures. Resilience supports this process by helping players recover emotionally from mistakes and maintain their confidence.

Rugby is a team sport that requires trust and communication. Resilient players contribute to a positive team environment by maintaining composure during tough matches and encouraging their teammates to do the same. Gritty players inspire others with their work ethic and determination, setting a standard for the entire team to follow.

Building Mental Toughness

The combination of resilience and grit forms the foundation of mental toughness—the ability to remain focused, composed, and determined in the face of challenges. Mental toughness is crucial in rugby, where players must navigate physical exhaustion, strategic shifts, and emotional highs and lows within a single game.

How to Develop Resilience and Grit in Rugby Players:

Encourage a Growth Mindset

A growth mindset—the belief that abilities can be developed through effort—is essential for building resilience and grit. Coaches and parents should praise effort over results, emphasizing the importance of learning from mistakes and striving for improvement.

Set Challenging but Achievable Goals

Setting realistic, incremental goals helps players stay motivated and focused. Achieving small milestones builds confidence and demonstrates the value of perseverance, while the occasional setback provides opportunities to practice resilience.

Practice Reflection and Visualization

Encourage players to reflect on their performances, identifying what went well and what could be improved. Visualization techniques can help them mentally rehearse successful plays and build confidence in their abilities, fostering both resilience and grit.

Build a Supportive Environment

A strong support network of coaches, teammates, and family members can bolster players' resilience and grit. Constructive feedback, encouragement, and shared experiences help players stay motivated and bounce back from adversity.

Teach Emotional Regulation

Emotional regulation strategies, such as deep breathing and mindfulness, equip players to manage stress and maintain focus during games. These skills are essential for resilience, enabling players to recover quickly from mistakes and stay composed in high-pressure situations.

Resilience and grit are necessary for young rugby players, helping them work through the ups and downs of the sport while striving for excellence. By understanding the differences between these qualities and actively developing them, players can enhance their performance, contribute to their team's success, and grow into well-rounded individuals both on and off the pitch.

The Science Behind a Resilient and Gritty Brain

Resilience and grit aren't just personality traits; they are abilities that can be developed with practice and an understanding of how your brain works.

When you face challenges or setbacks, your brain activates its stress response. A key area involved in this process is the prefrontal cortex, the front of your brain, which helps you think logically, plan, and manage emotions. If this part of your brain stays calm, you're better able to handle pressure during a tough rugby match or bounce back from a mistake, like a knock-on or missed tackle. Studies have shown that practices like mindfulness and reflection strengthen the prefrontal cortex, making you more resilient over time.

On the other hand, grit relies on your brain's reward system, especially the release of dopamine, a chemical that makes you feel good when you achieve goals. According to psychologist Angela Duckworth, setting long-term goals and sticking with them trains your brain to associate effort and persistence with rewards. This is why staying committed to daily rugby drills, even when it's hard, even when it's raining or snowing, builds grit—it rewires your brain to value persistence and hard work over instant success.

So, whether you're bouncing back from a tough loss or pushing yourself during training, know that every effort is making your brain stronger, more resilient, and grittier.

PLAYER PROFILE: ILONA MAHER
A True Example of Resilience and Grit

For young rugby players looking for inspiration, Ilona Maher is a name worth knowing. As a standout player for the USA Women's Rugby Sevens team, Ilona has shown how resilience and grit can help overcome challenges both on and off the pitch. Her journey to becoming one of the most recognizable names in women's rugby is filled with lessons about perseverance, adaptability, and mental strength.

Early Challenges and Career Switch

Ilona Maher's path to rugby wasn't typical. She grew up in Vermont, where rugby wasn't a common sport. Like many athletes, she started with other activities, including basketball and field hockey. Though she excelled in sports, her early focus was on a career in nursing. Transitioning from nursing to pursue rugby full-time was no easy decision. It required a leap of faith and the willingness to dedicate herself to a demanding and unfamiliar sport.

This bold career shift is a testament to Ilona's adaptability and belief in her abilities. She didn't let self-doubt or fear of failure hold her back. Instead, she committed to rugby wholeheartedly, quickly rising through the ranks to earn a spot on the USA Women's Rugby Sevens team.

Battling Through Injuries

Like many professional athletes, Ilona's journey hasn't been free from physical setbacks. Injuries are a part of rugby, a sport that demands both mental and physical toughness. Ilona has faced several injuries throughout her career, each time demonstrating incredible resilience in her recovery process.

For Ilona, these moments were not just about healing physically. Recovering from an injury often comes with mental challenges, such as staying positive during long rehabilitation periods and maintaining confidence in returning to peak performance. Ilona tackled these hurdles with determination, using setbacks as opportunities to grow stronger. Her comebacks have proven her ability to rise above adversity and return to the field as a formidable player.

Olympic Journey: Performing Under Pressure

One of the highlights of Ilona Maher's career was competing in the Tokyo 2020 Olympics. Representing your country on the world's biggest stage is a dream for many athletes, but it comes with immense pressure. For Ilona and the USA team, the competition was fierce, and while they didn't bring home a medal, Ilona's performance stood out. She was praised for her leadership, determination, and ability to give her all despite the challenges the team faced.

The 2024 Summer Olympics in Paris were a historic moment for Ilona Maher and the U.S. rugby sevens team, as they secured their first-ever Olympic medal in the sport. Maher, known for her powerful playing style and leadership, played a key role throughout the tournament. The team advanced through the group stage with strong performances, including Maher scoring in all three matches. After falling to New Zealand in the semifinals, the U.S. bounced back in the bronze medal match, defeating Australia in a thrilling contest. The victory not only cemented their place in American rugby history but also showcased the growing strength of women's rugby on the international stage.

Leading On and Off the Pitch
Ilona's influence extends beyond her performance on the rugby field. She is a vocal advocate for body positivity and mental health awareness, using her platform to inspire others. Her openness about her struggles and her ability to connect with fans on social media have made her a role model for young athletes everywhere.

By sharing her journey, Ilona reminds young players that setbacks, whether physical or emotional, are part of the process. She's proof that it's not about avoiding challenges but about how you respond to them. Her resilience off the pitch mirrors her toughness on it, making her an all-around inspiration.

Ilona's career is far from over, and her influence continues to grow. With each game, she proves that resilience and grit are essential qualities for success in rugby and life. Her journey reminds young players that the path to greatness isn't always smooth, but it's the challenges along the way that shape you into the athlete and person you're meant to be.

So, whether you're facing a tough loss, coming back from an injury, or simply trying to improve your game, look to Ilona Maher for inspiration. She's proof that with resilience and grit, you can overcome almost anything.

Conclusion: A Resilient & Gritty Player

Resilience and grit are more than just words—they are the foundation for tackling tough times, both on and off the pitch. In rugby, these qualities enable players to push through challenges, recover from setbacks, and relentlessly pursue their goals.

The stories of athletes like Ilona Maher demonstrate that resilience allows you to rise from adversity, while grit keeps you focused on long-term aspirations. These traits not only enhance performance on the field but also shape character, helping players grow into confident, determined individuals who can face life's challenges head-on.

To build resilience and grit, young rugby players must develop a growth mindset, set achievable goals, and reflect on their experiences. Support from coaches, teammates, and family creates an environment where these traits can thrive. Techniques like mindfulness, visualization, and emotional regulation are important tools that strengthen mental toughness and prepare players for the pressures of the game.

As you leave the pitch and reflect on your performance, remember this: success isn't just about the wins; it's about how you face the losses, adapt, and continue to move forward. With resilience and grit, you'll be the rugby player that coaches search for and fellow players look up to.

4 ACTIVITIES TO HELP YOU WITH DEVELOPING RESILIENCE & GRIT

#1 Complete a Tough Physical Challenge

Set a challenging goal, like completing a long-distance run or finishing a grueling fitness circuit. Push through even when it gets difficult, focusing on finishing rather than quitting.

Why it Works: Physical challenges build grit by teaching players to endure discomfort and persist despite fatigue. Overcoming these obstacles fosters mental toughness, instilling confidence that they can handle tough situations on the pitch.

#2 Embrace Productive Failure

Intentionally tackle something you find difficult, like perfecting a tricky pass or learning a new kicking technique. Focus on improving with each attempt, rather than avoiding mistakes.

Why it Works: Confronting failure teaches players to view setbacks as opportunities for growth rather than obstacles. This mindset fosters resilience and grit, enabling players to keep trying until they succeed.

#3 Create a Resilience Ritual

Develop a personal ritual to reset after mistakes, like clapping your hands, tapping your chest, or repeating a positive affirmation. Practice this ritual during training so it becomes second nature in games.

Why it Works: Rituals provide a tangible way to manage emotions and refocus after setbacks, promoting resilience. They also help players stay mentally grounded, preventing negative thoughts from spiraling out of control.

(#4) Celebrate Effort, Not Just Results

After practices and games, recognize effort by rewarding yourself or teammates for hard work, whether it's completing a tough drill or showing determination in a challenging scrimmage.

Why it Works: Celebrating effort reinforces the idea that hard work is valuable, regardless of the outcome. This strengthens grit by keeping players motivated through tough times and promotes resilience by shifting focus from setbacks to progress.

6

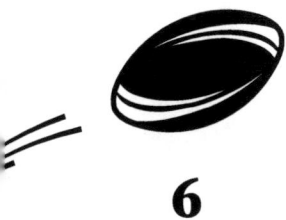

CLEARING THE RUCK:
Using Mindfulness for Focus and Performance

In rugby, just like in life, the ability to stay focused under pressure, bounce back from mistakes, and adapt to the flow of the game is crucial. Whether you're preparing for a scrum, tracking the ball in the air, or lining up a conversion, your mental game is just as important as your physical skills. Mindfulness—the practice of staying present and aware in the moment—can help young rugby players sharpen their focus, manage emotions, and make better decisions on the field.

What Is Mindfulness?

Mindfulness is the practice of paying attention to the present moment with purpose and without judgment. In rugby terms, it's about staying mentally grounded in the here and now rather than getting distracted by what just happened in the game or worrying about what might happen at the end of the game. For example, mindfulness could mean focusing on the feel of the ball in your hands during a pass, noticing your breath as you prepare for a kick, or tuning into the pace of the match without letting distractions throw you off your game.

Although mindfulness has its roots in meditation, it's now widely used in sports to help athletes develop mental clarity, resilience, and focus. For young rugby players, practicing mindfulness can mean learning to respond to situations on the pitch with calm and composure, even when the game gets intense. It's the mental equivalent of holding your ground during a tough ruck or staying locked in while taking a high ball.

Why Mindfulness Matters in Rugby

Rugby is a fast-paced, high-impact sport that requires players to think quickly, act decisively, and recover from setbacks in an instant. The pressure to perform can sometimes feel overwhelming, but mindfulness can help by equipping players with the mental tools to stay in control, no matter what the game throws at them.

Here are some key benefits of mindfulness for young rugby players:

Improved Focus and Concentration

Rugby is a game of constant movement, where players need to process multiple factors at the same time: the position of the ball, the alignment of teammates, the opposing team's strategy, and the coach's calls from the sideline. It's easy to get distracted, or overwhelmed by all the action.

Mindfulness helps players filter out distractions and focus on what truly matters in the moment. Think of it as mental conditioning: just as you build physical stamina through training, mindfulness builds your ability to stay mentally sharp from kickoff to the final whistle. This intense focus is what players often describe as "being in the zone"—a state of total engagement where every decision and movement feels natural and effortless.

Emotional Regulation

Rugby is an emotional sport, and young players often experience a rollercoaster of feelings during a match. Whether it's the frustration of a knock-on, the exhilaration of scoring a try, or the stress of defending in the dying minutes, these emotions can affect performance if not managed well.

Mindfulness teaches players to recognize and accept their emotions without being controlled by them. For example, if you feel frustration building after a missed tackle, mindfulness can help you acknowledge the feeling, let it go, and shift your focus back to the game. This ability to regulate emotions keeps you grounded and ensures that your next decision on the pitch is clear-headed rather than impulsive.

Building Resilience and Confidence

Setbacks are part of rugby. Whether it's losing a match, coming up off the deck from a hard tackle, or making a costly error, every player will face challenges. Mindfulness helps build resilience by teaching players to accept setbacks as a natural part of the game. Instead of dwelling on mistakes, a mindful player learns from them and moves forward with confidence.

In addition, mindfulness encourages self-compassion—treating yourself with kindness instead of harsh criticism when things go wrong. This positive mindset helps young players maintain their confidence and see challenges as opportunities for growth rather than failures.

Faster Reaction Times and Better Decision-Making

Rugby is a game of split-second decisions. Whether you're deciding to pass, kick, or run, the ability to stay calm and focused under pressure can make all the difference. Mindfulness helps players stay present in these high-pressure moments, enabling them to trust their instincts and react quickly to the unfolding game.

For instance, when faced with a charging defender, a mindful player can assess the situation clearly and act decisively— whether it's executing a perfect dummy pass, taking the tackle, or offloading the ball to a teammate. This clarity of mind reduces hesitation and leads to smarter, faster decisions on the field.

Accessing the "Flow State"

Many athletes strive to reach the "flow state"—a mental zone where they feel fully immersed in the game and everything seems to click effortlessly. In rugby, this might look like flawlessly reading the opposition's defense, timing your tackles perfectly, or executing a strategic play with precision. Mindfulness can help players access this flow state by quieting mental distractions and tuning into the rhythm of the match.

When you're in the flow state, you're not overthinking or worrying about outcomes. Instead, you're completely in sync with the game, which leads to the best performances. Practicing mindfulness makes it easier to tap into this state, allowing you to play with confidence, skill, and optimism.

How to Start Practicing Mindfulness

Mindfulness doesn't require special equipment or hours of practice. Simple techniques like focusing on your breath, using visualization, or practicing body awareness can make a big difference. For example, before a match, take a moment to breathe deeply and visualize yourself playing confidently and calmly. During the game, bring your focus back to the present moment by noticing the feel of the ground beneath your boots or the sound of your teammates' voices, really connecting to your senses.

By incorporating mindfulness into your training and match preparation, you'll not only enhance your rugby performance but also develop valuable skills that can benefit you off the field. Staying present, managing emotions, and bouncing back from setbacks are qualities that will serve you well in all areas of life.

The Science Behind Mindfulness for Young Rugby Players

Mindfulness has a wonderful impact on the brain, and understanding the science behind it can help young rugby players appreciate its benefits on and off the pitch. Neuroscience shows that mindfulness strengthens the brain areas responsible for focus, decision-making, and emotional regulation—key skills for rugby players.

One major area impacted by mindfulness is the prefrontal cortex, the part of the brain that helps with decision-making and staying focused. For rugby players, a strong prefrontal cortex means staying sharp during intense scrums or making quick decisions when the opposing team is on the attack. Studies have shown that mindfulness increases the density of gray matter in this region, making it easier to block out distractions and focus on executing game plans.

Mindfulness also calms the amygdala, the brain's stress center. Staying composed after a tough tackle or a turnover is crucial. By practicing mindfulness, players can reduce stress, control frustration, and focus on the next play instead of dwelling on mistakes.

Lastly, mindfulness strengthens the connection between the prefrontal cortex and the amygdala, enabling better emotional control under pressure. This balance helps rugby players stay cool-headed, think clearly, and perform at their best—even when the game is on the line.

PLAYER PROFILE: JOHNNY SEXTON
Mindfulness to Maintain Mastery

For rugby players dreaming of greatness, there's no better role model than Johnny Sexton, a rugby legend whose mental game is as sharp as his on-field skills. Born in Dublin, Ireland, Sexton grew up in a family passionate about sports. His early years were spent playing rugby in his local community, where he showed a natural flair for the game. Despite his talent, his journey to the top wasn't without its challenges, and Sexton's use of mindfulness has been a key factor in overcoming adversity and thriving under pressure.

Early Life and Rugby Beginnings
Johnny Sexton was born on July 11, 1985, and raised in Rathgar, a suburb of Dublin. Growing up, Sexton idolized Irish rugby legends and spent countless hours perfecting his kicking skills in the garden. His natural talent and determination were evident early on, and he quickly became a standout player at St. Mary's College, where he balanced academics and rugby.

Despite his success at the schoolboy level, Sexton faced setbacks when trying to break into professional rugby. Initially, he struggled to secure his place in the Leinster senior squad, battling self-doubt and inconsistent performances. For many players, these challenges could have derailed a promising career, but Sexton's resilience and mental toughness helped him persevere.

Sexton's breakthrough came in 2009 when he led Leinster to a historic Heineken Cup victory, but even after this career-defining moment, he continued to face immense pressure. As Ireland's starting fly-half, Sexton's role required him to make split-second decisions, kick crucial penalties, and guide his team under intense scrutiny. The weight of expectations, combined with injuries and the natural ups and downs of elite sport, pushed Sexton to seek ways to strengthen his mental game.

Mindfulness became a cornerstone of his approach. By practicing mindfulness, Sexton learned how to stay present, manage stress, and remain composed in high-pressure moments. Whether preparing for a penalty kick or leading Ireland in the Six Nations, mindfulness allowed him to block out distractions and focus on the task at hand.

Sexton has spoken about the importance of mindfulness in his life, emphasizing how it helps him bounce back from setbacks and approach challenges with a clear mind. For example, after tough losses or personal criticism, Sexton uses mindfulness techniques like deep breathing and meditation to process his emotions and refocus on his goals.

Mindfulness on the Pitch

On the field, Sexton's mindfulness practice has translated into extraordinary composure. As a fly-half, he's often the player calling the shots, making tactical decisions, and executing plays under intense pressure. His ability to stay calm and think clearly in chaotic situations is a testament to his mental training.

One of Sexton's most memorable performances came during the 2018 Six Nations Grand Slam campaign, where he kicked a last-minute drop goal against France. This iconic moment highlighted his unshakeable focus, precision, and ability to thrive under pressure—all skills that mindfulness has helped him develop.

Johnny Sexton's story is proof that success in rugby is about more than physical skill; it's about mastering your mindset. By practicing mindfulness, Sexton has built the mental resilience needed to handle adversity and perform at the highest level.

For young players, Sexton's journey is a reminder that challenges are part of the game, but with the right tools and mindset, you can overcome them. Whether it's staying calm before a match, letting go of mistakes, or staying focused during a tough game, mindfulness can help you unlock your full potential—just like it has for one of rugby's greatest players.

Conclusion: Clearing the Ruck and Your Mind with Mindfulness

Mindfulness is a magical tool that young rugby players can use to sharpen their focus, control their emotions, and enhance their performance on the pitch. Just like mastering a long spin pass or perfecting your kick to touch, mindfulness requires practice and dedication—but the rewards can be game-changing.

As Johnny Sexton's story demonstrates, the mental side of rugby is as crucial as the physical. Sexton's ability to stay present and composed under pressure is not just a testament to his skill but also to his commitment to developing a strong mental game. His use of mindfulness has allowed him to overcome setbacks, stay focused during high-stakes moments, and inspire countless young players to follow in his footsteps.

For young rugby players, adopting mindfulness is like clearing a ruck: it helps you focus on the task at hand, clear away distractions, and create the space you need to succeed. By practicing simple techniques like deep breathing, visualization, or paying attention to the present moment, you can train your mind to stay calm and focused, no matter the situation.

Remember, rugby is a sport of highs and lows. There will be missed tackles, dropped balls, and games that don't go your way. But with mindfulness, you can learn to accept these challenges, recover quickly, and keep moving forward. Whether you're preparing for a kick, lining up for a tackle, or strategizing for the next play, staying mentally grounded will help you perform at your best.

So, step onto the pitch with confidence, knowing that mindfulness can be your secret weapon. By embracing the present moment and staying mentally strong, you'll not only improve your game but also grow as a player and person, ready to tackle whatever comes your way.

4 ACTIVITIES TO HELP YOU WITH DEVELOPING MINDFULNESS

#1 Breath Awareness Drill

Before practice or a match, take 2–3 minutes to focus solely on your breathing. Sit or stand in a relaxed position and close your eyes. Breathe in deeply through your nose for a count of four, hold for four counts, and exhale through your mouth for six counts. As you breathe, focus entirely on the sensation of air entering and leaving your body. If your mind wanders, gently bring it back to your breath.

Why It Works: Breath awareness calms your nervous system by activating the parasympathetic (relaxation) response. This reduces pre-match jitters and increases focus. By building your ability to concentrate on your breath, you also train your mind to stay present during intense game situations, helping you react more effectively under pressure.

#2 Silent Solo Practice

Set aside time to practice a rugby skill, such as kicking or tackling, in silence. Focus entirely on the mechanics of your movements and the feedback from your body. For example, during kicking practice, notice the placement of your foot, the motion of your leg, and the contact with the ball.

Why It Works: Silent solo practice helps eliminate distractions and improves your technical precision. By concentrating on the details of your movements, you build muscle memory and increase your confidence in executing skills during games. It also reinforces the importance of staying present in the moment.

#3 Mindful Ball Handling

Spend 5–10 minutes handling the rugby ball in a quiet space. Focus on how the ball feels in your hands—its texture, weight, and shape. Slowly pass the ball back and forth between your hands, noticing every movement. If your mind starts to wander, gently redirect it to the sensations of holding and moving the ball.

Why It Works: This activity strengthens your connection to the ball and trains you to stay present. By engaging your senses, you heighten awareness and block out distractions. This improved focus translates directly to better ball handling during games, especially in high-pressure moments when precision is key.

#4 Post-Game Reflection

After a match, sit quietly for a few minutes and reflect on your performance. Identify moments when you stayed focused and times when you were distracted or emotional. Acknowledge these moments without judgment and think about what you can learn from them. Pair this reflection with a few deep breaths to help you process your thoughts.

Why It Works: Post-game reflection helps you develop self-awareness and emotional regulation. By analyzing your mindset during the game, you can identify areas for improvement and celebrate successes. This habit encourages growth and helps you approach future matches with a clearer and more resilient mindset.

7

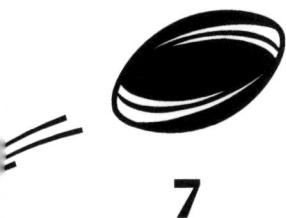

EYES ON THE TRY LINE:
Aligning Your Goals with Your Training and Play

Every great rugby match begins with a solid game plan. From executing set pieces to organizing the backline, having a clear strategy is essential for success on the pitch. But success in rugby doesn't just happen during the 80 minutes of play—it's built on countless hours of preparation, training, and mental focus. That's where goal setting comes into play. Just like a coach lays out the tactics for the team, you, as an aspiring rugby player, can use goals to guide your growth, improve your skills, and achieve your dreams.

Goal setting is a tool used by top athletes to maintain focus, stay motivated, and track progress. It's the difference between aimlessly kicking the ball downfield and targeting the perfect spot for a lineout. Without goals, it's easy to lose sight of what you're working toward and how to get there. Goals give you direction, purpose, and a clear sense of achievement as you improve.

However, not all goals are created equal. In rugby, there's a structure to every phase of play: from setting up the scrum to executing the backline move that leads to a try. Similarly, there are different types of goals, each serving a unique purpose in your development. These are process goals, performance goals, and outcome goals. Let's break them down using rugby examples to better understand how to apply each to your game.

Process Goals: The Foundation of Every Play

In rugby, every phase of play begins with the fundamentals. You don't score a try without first securing the ball in the ruck, and you can't execute a perfect pass without mastering your hand position and follow-through. Process goals focus on these small, controllable actions that build the foundation for success.

Process goals are about what you need to do every day to improve. For example, a process goal might be: "Practice my passing accuracy for 15 minutes after every training session." You control this goal entirely—it doesn't depend on the outcome of a game or your teammates' performance.

By focusing on process goals, you develop the skills and habits that set you up for long-term success. Whether it's working on your tackling form, perfecting your kicking technique, or improving your fitness through regular conditioning, process goals are the building blocks of your rugby journey.

Performance Goals: Hitting Your Personal Best

While process goals focus on the how, performance goals focus on the what. Performance goals measure your individual performance in specific areas of the game and challenge you to achieve measurable progress. Performance goals are all about pushing yourself to new levels of excellence.

For instance, a performance goal could be: "Complete 90% of my tackles in the next match," or "Achieve a 50-meter kick to touch during practice." These goals focus on your personal achievements and are measured against a standard you set for yourself. They don't depend on whether your team wins or loses; instead, they're about evaluating your own performance on the field.

Performance goals help you track improvement and give you targets to strive for. They're like setting a benchmark in the gym—each time you hit a new personal best, it's a clear sign of your progress.

Outcome Goals: Aiming for the Try Line

Outcome goals are the big-picture objectives that focus on the final result. They're the equivalent of scoring a try, winning a tournament, or making the starting lineup. These goals are often what motivate us the most—they represent the ultimate achievements we dream about as rugby players.

For example, an outcome goal might be: "Win the regional championship with my team," or "Get selected for the provincial rugby squad." Outcome goals are exciting and inspiring, but they're also influenced by factors outside your control, such as your teammates' performance, the referee's decisions, or even the weather on match day.

While outcome goals can drive motivation, relying too heavily on them can lead to frustration if things don't go as planned. That's why it's essential to balance them with process and performance goals. By focusing on what you can control—your preparation and performance—you'll be better equipped to achieve the outcomes you're aiming for.

Bringing It All Together

Imagine you're preparing for a crucial rugby match. Your outcome goal might be to win the game and advance to the next round of the competition. To achieve that, you set a performance goal: "Make at least 8 successful tackles and 2 clean breaks during the match." But how do you ensure you're ready to meet that target? By focusing on process goals, such as: "Practice my defensive positioning and tackle technique for 20 minutes at every training session this week."

When you align these three types of goals—process, performance, and outcome—you create a powerful game plan that sets you up for success both on and off the field. Process goals build your skills and habits, performance goals challenge your abilities, and outcome goals inspire you to reach for greatness.

Goal setting is much like rugby itself: a mix of strategy, preparation, and execution. By understanding and using these three types of goals, you'll not only improve your game but also build the mental toughness and discipline needed to thrive in rugby and beyond. So, lace up your boots, grab your ball, and start setting goals that will help you cross the try line to success.

The Science Behind Goal Setting for Young Rugby Players

Setting goals is like having a game plan for your brain. It gives you a clear direction and helps you know what to work toward. But did you know there's actual science behind how goals can help you perform better on the rugby field? Let's break it down.

Your brain loves goals because they give it something exciting to focus on. When you set a goal, your brain starts working like a coach. It creates a plan, tracks progress, and celebrates wins. But here's the trick: not all goals are created equal. That's why focusing on process goals is super important.

Process Goals

Imagine you want to score more tries this season. That's a great outcome goal—what you hope to achieve. However, process goals focus on what you need to do to get there. For example, you could set a process goal to practice your sidestep for 15 minutes every day or improve your sprinting technique three times a week. These smaller steps help you get better every day and keep you focused on things you can control, like effort and technique.

Why Does This Help Your Brain?

Your brain loves progress. Every time you hit a small goal—like perfecting a passing drill—it releases a chemical called dopamine. Dopamine is often called the "feel-good chemical" because it gives you a sense of happiness and accomplishment. It's like your brain's way of saying, "Great job! Keep going!"

This boost of dopamine makes you want to work even harder. It also helps your brain create strong connections, which means you'll remember what you've learned and improve faster. By focusing on process goals, you get more opportunities to celebrate progress and train your brain to enjoy hard work.

How Does This Help You in Rugby?

When you focus on small, achievable goals, you build confidence. Instead of worrying about the final score, you're giving your best effort to improve specific skills. Over time, all those small wins add up to big improvements, like faster running, stronger tackles, and better teamwork.

So, remember, young rugby players: set process goals, celebrate your progress, and let dopamine do its magic. With a focused mind and a solid plan, you'll be an unstoppable force on the field!

PLAYER PROFILE: ANTOINE DUPONT
Goal Setting for Olympic Glory

Growing up in the rugby heartland of southern France, Antoine Dupont was introduced to the sport of rugby at the tender age of five, playing for his local club, Magnoac FC. His talent was evident early on, and by the age of 15, he had joined the youth ranks of FC Auch, a club renowned for nurturing young talent. This period was instrumental in building his skills and understanding of the game, laying a solid foundation for his future.

Dupont's exceptional performances at the youth level caught the attention of top-tier French clubs, leading to his professional debut with Castres Olympique in 2014. His dynamic playing style, characterized by swift decision-making and explosive runs, quickly made him a standout player. In 2017, he signed with Toulouse, one of Europe's premier rugby clubs. At Toulouse, Dupont's career flourished; he played a pivotal role in securing multiple domestic titles and was instrumental in their European Champions Cup victory. His performance on the field earned him a place in the French national team, where he further solidified his reputation as one of the world's leading scrum-halves.

Strategic Goal Setting and Transition to Rugby Sevens

In the wake of a heart-wrenching quarter-final loss to South Africa during the 2023 Rugby World Cup, Dupont sought new avenues to channel his competitive spirit and achieve sporting excellence. Identifying the 2024 Paris Olympic Games as a unique opportunity, he set a formidable goal: to transition from rugby union (15s) to rugby sevens and secure an Olympic gold medal on home soil.

Dupont's unwavering commitment to his goal culminated in a historic performance at the 2024 Paris Olympics. His leadership and skills were on full display as he guided France to a 28-7 victory over the two-time defending champions, Fiji, in the rugby sevens final. Dupont's contributions were pivotal, including scoring two tries and orchestrating key plays that secured France's first-ever Olympic gold in rugby sevens.

Reflection on Goal Setting and Legacy

Antoine Dupont's journey demonstrates the power of strategic goal-setting in achieving athletic excellence. By setting clear, measurable objectives and systematically working towards them, he successfully navigated the challenges of transitioning between rugby formats and reached the pinnacle of success on the Olympic stage.

His story serves as an inspiration to athletes worldwide, illustrating that with deliberate planning, adaptability, and unwavering dedication, even the most ambitious goals are within reach. As Dupont continues his career, his legacy is not only defined by his on-field achievements but also by his approach to personal and professional growth through goal setting.

Conclusion: Eyes on the Try Line: Aligning Your Goals with Your Training and Play

As young rugby players, setting goals is like crafting your game plan—it helps you navigate challenges, celebrate victories, and continuously improve. Whether you're mastering your tackling technique, improving your passing, or dreaming of scoring the winning try in a championship match, goal setting can guide you every step of the way.

The beauty of goal setting lies in its structure. Process goals keep your focus on the little things, like practicing your sidestep or improving your fitness, which are entirely in your control. These daily actions build the foundation for bigger achievements. Performance goals push you to new personal bests, like nailing 90% of your tackles in a game. Finally, outcome goals inspire you with the ultimate vision, like winning a tournament or making the provincial squad.

Remember, the key is balance. By focusing on process goals, you'll enjoy the journey and celebrate the small wins that keep you motivated. Performance goals will challenge you to improve, while outcome goals will remind you why you're putting in all that effort. Together, these goals create a powerful strategy that prepares you for success on the pitch and beyond.

Like a well-executed play, achieving your goals requires patience, practice, and teamwork. Don't be afraid to adjust your goals along the way—rugby is a game of adaptability, and so is life. Your goals are waiting, and with the right mindset and effort, there's nothing stopping you from crossing over and celebrating your success.

3 ACTIVITIES TO HELP YOU WITH YOUR GOAL-SETTING

#1) Create a Goal Ladder

Write down a big rugby goal at the top of a piece of paper, such as "Make the school rugby team." Underneath, list smaller, step-by-step goals leading to it, like "Practice tackling drills three times a week," "Improve passing accuracy to 80%," and "Run 2 km daily to build endurance." Add dates to each step to create a timeline and cross off goals as you achieve them.

Why It Works: A goal ladder breaks a big dream into manageable, actionable steps. It helps players avoid feeling overwhelmed and builds confidence as they see progress. Crossing off smaller goals triggers a sense of accomplishment, releasing dopamine, which boosts motivation and reinforces positive habits.

#2) Journal Your Progress

Keep a rugby-specific journal where you write down your daily training efforts, strengths, and areas for improvement. At the end of each week, reflect on what went well and set a small goal for the next week, like improving speed, accuracy, or endurance.

Why It Works: Journaling helps players track their progress and maintain accountability. It creates a space for self-reflection, allowing them to identify patterns, celebrate small victories, and stay motivated. Regular reflection ensures goals remain relevant and helps players adjust their strategies as needed.

(#3) Goal Setting with a Partner

Find a teammate and share your personal goals for the upcoming season or week. Whether it's improving your footwork, getting stronger, or nailing your tackling technique, talk through your goals together. Then, work as a team to come up with specific actions to make those goals happen, like dedicating extra time to training or focusing on specific drills. You'll want to check in with each other regularly to track progress, offer encouragement, and hold each other accountable.

Why It Works: When you set goals with a partner, you've got someone to keep you motivated and remind you to stay on track. It adds accountability—when you know someone else is counting on you to follow through, it's easier to stay committed. Plus, watching your partner improve can push you to give your best effort, too! This collaboration builds stronger teamwork, while also making your goals feel more achievable because you're working together toward success.

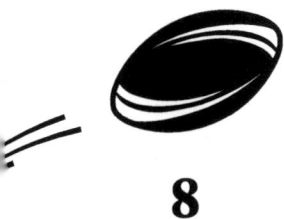

8

GAINING ADVANTAGE:
Keeping Positive Self-Talk in Play

When you're out on the rugby field, your body needs to be strong to run, tackle, and pass effectively. But, as you're learning, your mind is just as important as your muscles. One of the most powerful tools you can use to improve your mental game is positive self-talk. Positive self-talk is like having your own personal coach in your head, cheering you on and guiding you through challenges. It's when you say encouraging things to yourself, either quietly in your mind or out loud. These words can help you stay calm, focused, and confident, even during the toughest moments of the match.

For example, imagine you miss a tackle. Instead of thinking, "I'm so bad at this," positive self-talk might sound like, "It's okay, I'll get stuck in on the next one," or, "It's one small mistake—stay in the game." It's all about replacing those unhelpful thoughts with ones that keep you motivated and ready to play at your best.

Why Positive Self-Talk Matters in Rugby

In rugby, things can change in an instant. Mistakes happen, and games can get stressful. How you handle those moments can make all the difference. When you use positive self-talk, you stay confident in your abilities and believe you can handle whatever comes your way. Encouraging yourself helps you recover quickly from setbacks, whether it's a missed pass or a lost scrum, and keeps your head in the game. It also helps you handle pressure, like making a crucial kick or defending your try line, because staying calm leads to better decisions.

This way of thinking doesn't just help you feel good—it has real benefits for your performance. When you talk to yourself in a positive way, you're more likely to stay focused on your strengths and what's possible. Positive self-talk also reduces the stress of high-pressure situations, like a close game or a tough opponent, and helps you stay in control of your emotions. Over time, it builds resilience, allowing you to push through challenges, whether it's extra fitness drills or recovering from a loss. It also improves team spirit; when you're kind to yourself, it's easier to encourage your teammates too, spreading a positive energy or vibe throughout the team.

How Positive Self-Talk Works

The way positive self-talk works is simple but powerful. Your brain soaks up whatever you tell it. If you keep saying negative things, like "I'm not good enough" or "I'll mess up," your brain starts to believe it. But when you feed it positive messages, like "I'm strong" or "I've practiced this," your brain responds by helping you perform better.

For instance, before a game, you might feel nervous. Using positive self-talk, such as "I've trained hard, and I'm ready," sets you up for success by calming your nerves and focusing your mind. During a match, staying present is crucial. A simple phrase like "Next play, stay sharp" keeps you focused on what you need to do instead of dwelling on mistakes. After the game, reflecting positively is just as important. Instead of thinking, "I missed that tackle," you could say, "I gave my best effort today and learned something I need to work on."

Building Positive Self-Talk into Your Routine

Starting to use positive self-talk is easier than you might think. One way is to come up with a few power phrases, like "I can do this" or "Keep pushing." These are phrases you can repeat to yourself before, during, or after a game. When negative thoughts pop into your head, try to notice them and replace them with positive ones. For example, if you catch yourself thinking, "I'm bad at passing," reframe it to, "I'm improving my passing every day."

You can also practice positive self-talk during training by encouraging yourself during drills. For example, remind yourself to "stay focused" or "take it one step at a time." Visualization is another helpful tool. Picture yourself making a great tackle or scoring a try while repeating positive phrases like "I'm a great rugby player." Even encouraging your teammates with positive words helps create a supportive and uplifting environment that boosts everyone's confidence.

Imagine this: before a game, you remind yourself, "I've worked hard all week, and I'm ready to play my best." During the match, you miss a tackle, but instead of getting upset, you tell yourself, "That's just one play—I'll make the next one count." When you start to feel tired, you think, "Keep pushing—you're almost there." In the final minutes, when the pressure is on, you stay calm and focused by saying, "I know what to do, time to lock in."

Positive self-talk is a game-changer for young rugby players. It helps you stay confident, recover quickly from mistakes, and handle the pressures of the game with a strong and steady mindset. Just like practicing your passing or tackling, training your mind to use positive words takes effort and time. But the more you do it, the easier it becomes—and the better you'll play.

So remember, the way you talk to yourself matters. Be your own biggest supporter, and watch how it transforms your game and your life on and off the field.

The Science of Positive Self-Talk

Positive self-talk is not just about feeling good—it's rooted in neuroscience and psychology. When rugby players use encouraging language with themselves, it activates the brain's reward system. This releases neurotransmitters like dopamine, which enhance focus and motivation. By replacing negative thoughts with positive ones, players train their brains to approach challenges with confidence and resilience.

Negative self-talk triggers the brain's stress response, increasing cortisol levels. This can make players feel anxious and less capable of handling pressure during games. Positive self-talk, on the other hand, helps regulate these stress responses. It engages the prefrontal cortex, the area responsible for decision-making and concentration, helping players stay calm and make better choices on the field.

Research also highlights how positive self-talk influences physical performance. Studies show that athletes who use motivational phrases can compete longer and recover more effectively from fatigue. This could mean the difference between lasting all the way through an intense match or asking for a sub, the difference between bouncing back after a tough tackle, or staying down on the pitch.

PLAYER PROFILE: JONNY WILKINSON
Mastering the Mind

Jonny Wilkinson is one of the greatest rugby players ever, not just because of his amazing skills but also because of his strong mental game. What made Jonny so special was his ability to stay positive and focused, even when the pressure was intense. He used positive self-talk to help him perform at his best, and it's a skill that any young rugby player can learn.

From a Kid with Big Dreams to a Rugby Star
Jonny Wilkinson was born on May 25, 1979, in Frimley, England. Like many kids, he loved sports, and rugby quickly became his favorite. He worked super hard to get better and joined the Newcastle Falcons when he was just 18 years old. That same year, he got picked to play for England's national team. Can you imagine representing your country as a teenager?

Jonny became known for his incredible kicking, his smart plays, and his dedication to the sport. He practiced for hours every day to perfect his skills, and his hard work paid off big time.

The most famous moment of Jonny's career happened in 2003 during the Rugby World Cup. England was playing Australia in the final. The score was tied, and the game was in extra time. With just seconds left, Jonny made a perfect drop goal to win the match. That kick didn't just win the game—it made Jonny a hero to rugby fans everywhere.

Over his career, Jonny scored 1,246 points in 97 games for England, becoming one of the highest-scoring players in history. He also had a successful career playing for Newcastle Falcons and Toulon, a French team.

How Jonny Used Positive Self-Talk

Jonny didn't just practice kicking and passing; he also trained his mind. He's talked about how his thoughts could sometimes be negative, like telling himself, "You're not good enough" or "What if you mess up?" But instead of letting those thoughts take over, Jonny learned to use positive self-talk to stay confident and focused.

Positive self-talk is like being your own cheerleader. Instead of thinking about what might go wrong, you remind yourself of what you can do. Jonny would tell himself things like, "You've got this," or "Focus on the next kick." By doing this, he stayed calm and didn't let the pressure get to him.

He also treated his inner voice like a teammate. If the voice in his head was being negative, he'd ask, "Would I talk to a teammate like this?" If the answer was no, he'd change what he was saying to himself.

Lots of rugby players are strong and skilled, but Jonny stood out because of his mental toughness. When the game was on the line, he was the player everyone could count on. He wasn't just playing against other teams—he was also overcoming his own doubts and fears.

Even after he retired, Jonny has continued to talk about how important it is to take care of your mental health. He shares his story to help others, showing that even the best players face challenges but can overcome them with the right mindset.

Jonny's story shows that rugby isn't just about strength and speed—it's also about your mind. By practicing positive self-talk, you can stay confident and focused, no matter what challenges come your way. The next time you're on the field and feeling nervous, try saying to yourself, "I can do this," or "I've practiced for this moment."

Like Jonny Wilkinson, you can be the kind of player who stays calm under pressure and always gives their best. Who knows? Maybe one day, you'll have your own legendary rugby moment!

Conclusion: The Power of Positive Self-Talk

As a young rugby player, you have so many opportunities to improve, both physically and mentally. Positive self-talk is a powerful tool to help you reach your full potential. Just like your body needs to be strong and well-trained to perform at your best, your mind needs to be strong, too. By using positive self-talk, you can boost your confidence, overcome challenges, and stay focused during tough moments in a game.

Remember that every great rugby player, like Jonny Wilkinson, didn't just rely on their skills— they also relied on their mindset. Jonny's ability to stay calm, focused, and positive in high-pressure moments helped him become one of the best players in the world. When you use positive self-talk, you're training your mind to be just as strong as your body. When you make a mistake, instead of getting frustrated, positive self-talk helps you stay in the game and move on. It helps you focus on the next play, not the one that's already passed.

Building positive self-talk into your routine can be a game-changer. By practicing every day, whether it's during practice or while you're on the field, you'll start to believe in yourself more. When you use encouraging words like "I can do this," or "I've got this," your brain learns to stay calm and focused. As a result, you'll perform better, recover faster, and feel more confident. Whether it's kicking the winning points or making a big tackle, positive self-talk can help you rise to the occasion.

You don't have to be perfect at it from the start. Just like with any skill, positive self-talk takes time to master. Start small and be patient with yourself. You'll notice that the more you use it, the easier it becomes, and before you know it, it'll be an automatic part of your mental game. So, the next time you face a tough moment, remember to be your own biggest supporter. With the right mindset, you'll be ready to take on any challenge that comes your way.

3 ACTIVITIES TO HELP YOU DEVELOP AND INCREASE POSITIVE SELF-TALK

#1 Mental Rehearsal for Key Skills

Before performing a key skill, like a kick or a tackle, take a moment to mentally rehearse the action while saying positive self-talk phrases. For instance, before a kick, you could say "I've practiced this kick a thousand times" (motivational) and "Focus on your follow-through" (instructional).

Why it Works: This activity works because mental rehearsal allows your brain to reinforce the steps needed for successful execution. Pairing it with self-talk gives your mind a clear direction, boosting confidence and ensuring that you stay focused on the task. By reinforcing these actions in your mind, you're preparing to perform them well when it counts.

#2 Challenge Yourself with New Goals

Set small, achievable goals for each practice, such as "I will focus on my tackles today" (instructional) or "I am going to work hard and push myself" (motivational). During the practice, whenever you achieve a goal, celebrate it with positive self-talk, such as "I nailed that tackle" (motivational) or "I was focused and kept my technique sharp" (instructional).

Why it Works: This activity works because it combines goal-setting with positive reinforcement. Achieving small goals boosts your confidence, and positive self-talk helps you acknowledge and internalize your successes. By linking positive self-talk to your goals, you keep yourself motivated to achieve more.

(#3) Use Self-Talk During Pre-Game Routines

Before every match, establish a pre-game self-talk routine where you repeat empowering statements like "I'm ready for this challenge" (motivational) and "Focus on the fundamentals" (instructional). You can even practice specific actions you want to excel at, like tackling or kicking.

Why it Works: This activity works because pre-game routines help settle nerves and boost confidence. By combining specific self-talk with your pre-game rituals, you prime your brain for a strong performance and put yourself in a positive mindset before the match begins. This type of mental preparation helps you feel more calm, focused, and ready to perform your best.

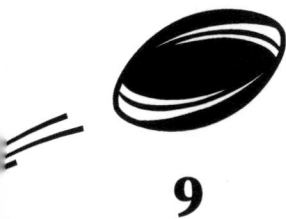

9

TRY-TIME:
Rituals and Routines for Gameday Greatness

Stepping onto the rugby field can be both exciting and nerve-wracking, especially for young players. There's the roar of the crowd, the adrenaline pumping through your veins, and the pressure to perform. While skill and fitness play vital roles in how you play, there's another secret weapon that can give you an edge: pre-game routines and rituals. These aren't just habits; they're powerful tools that help rugby players prepare mentally, physically, and emotionally for the challenges ahead.

What Are Rituals and Routines?

In rugby, pre-game rituals and routines are specific actions or sequences players follow before a match. A routine is a series of planned steps, like warming up, stretching, or practicing kicking. A ritual, on the other hand, often carries a personal or symbolic meaning, like tapping your boots together before stepping onto the field or wearing a lucky pair of socks.

Routines focus on preparation and performance, ensuring your body and mind are ready for the game. Rituals, though more personal, can boost confidence and provide a sense of control in high-pressure situations. Together, these habits set the stage for success, helping players feel focused, calm, and game-ready.

Why Are They Important?

Pre-game routines and rituals aren't just about getting ready to play—they're about creating a winning mindset. Here are a few reasons why they're so important for young rugby players:

Building Consistency: Rugby is unpredictable, with sudden tackles, fast passes, and unexpected plays. A consistent pre-game routine provides stability and familiarity, grounding you in the chaos of game day.

Managing Nerves: Feeling nervous before a game is natural, but too much anxiety can hurt your performance. A calming ritual, like deep breathing or repeating a positive phrase, can ease nerves and keep you focused.

Boosting Confidence: Rituals remind players of their hard work and preparation. For example, lacing up your boots the same way before every match can serve as a mental cue that you're ready to give your best.

Improving Focus: Pre-game routines help block out distractions, like the noise of the crowd or pressure from the competition, allowing you to concentrate on what matters most: playing your game.

The effectiveness of routines and rituals is backed by both science and experience. Routines help prepare your brain for action by creating a mental roadmap for what's to come. They activate the prefrontal cortex, the part of your brain responsible for focus and decision-making, and reduce the activity of the amygdala, which is linked to stress and fear. This means you can think clearly and perform under pressure.

Rituals also have a psychological impact. Studies show that personal rituals reduce anxiety and improve performance. They work by creating a sense of control and familiarity, even in unpredictable situations. Whether it's singing a song in your head or doing a specific warm-up drill, these small actions can make a big difference in how you feel—and play.

Professional rugby players are masters of pre-game preparation. They know the value of a solid routine and rely on rituals to help them perform their best. Here are a few examples:

Jonny Wilkinson, one of the greatest rugby players of all time, had a famously detailed kicking routine. Before every kick, he would align himself with the ball, crouch slightly, and focus intensely on his target. This ritual not only ensured consistency but also helped him stay calm during high-pressure moments, like his legendary drop goal in the 2003 Rugby World Cup final.

Richie McCaw, the legendary All Blacks captain, would visualize the game during his pre-match routine. By mentally walking through different scenarios, he prepared himself for anything that could happen on the field. Visualization is a powerful tool that young players can use to build confidence and readiness.

Emily Scarratt, a top player in women's rugby, often talks about the importance of having a clear routine before games. From eating the right pre-game meal to listening to her favorite music, she uses these habits to feel energized and focused.

These players didn't stumble upon their routines by chance. They developed them through practice and experimentation, finding what worked best for their minds and bodies. Building a pre-game routine doesn't have to be complicated. Start by thinking about what helps you feel calm and confident before a game. Your routine might include:

Physical Preparation: Warm-ups, stretches, and light drills to get your body ready.

Mental Focus: Visualization, breathing exercises, or positive self-talk to calm nerves and build confidence.

Symbolic Rituals: Personal actions, like putting on your jersey in a specific way or listening to a favorite song.

Remember, your routine is unique to you. What works for your teammate might not work for you, and that's okay. The key is consistency—practice your routine before every game so it becomes second nature. So, whether it's a quick pep talk to yourself, a favorite playlist, or a special warm-up drill, find the rituals and routines that work for you. With practice, they'll become your secret weapon for rugby success.

Why Routines Matter to Your Brain

Routines and rituals aren't just helpful habits—they're brain-boosting tools that enhance focus, reduce stress, and improve performance. When you follow a routine, your brain enters a predictable sequence of events. This predictability reduces uncertainty, calming the amygdala, the brain's "alarm system" responsible for stress and anxiety. At the same time, routines activate the prefrontal cortex, the part of your brain responsible for planning, focus, and decision-making. This dual effect allows you to stay calm under pressure and concentrate on playing your best rugby.

Rituals, while often symbolic, provide an additional layer of support. Research has shown that even small, deliberate actions, such as tying your boots in a specific way or visualizing success, create a sense of control in uncertain situations. This sense of control helps regulate cortisol, the stress hormone, preventing it from impairing performance.

For aspiring rugby players, routines are especially important because they create consistency in preparation, which leads to confidence on game day.

By establishing routines and rituals, you train your brain to shift into a focused and confident state before each game. This mental preparation ensures you're ready to tackle challenges and perform at your peak.

Sophie de Goede is more than just a rugby player—she is an inspiration for young athletes everywhere. As the captain of Canada's women's rugby team, Sophie's story is one of hard work, family tradition, and a commitment to excellence. She has shown that routines and rituals can be powerful tools for success, both on and off the field.

A Family Full of Rugby Legends

Sophie grew up in a family where rugby wasn't just a sport—it was a way of life. Her parents, Stephanie White and Hans de Goede are Canadian rugby legends. Stephanie captained the Canadian women's rugby team, while Hans led the men's team. With such a strong rugby legacy, it's no surprise that Sophie found herself drawn to the sport.

But rugby wasn't the only sport Sophie played. She also excelled at basketball and volleyball, showing that being a well-rounded athlete can help build important skills like teamwork, focus, and resilience. Growing up, Sophie learned the value of discipline and hard work from her parents, who encouraged her to always give her best effort, no matter the challenge.

Building Powerful Rituals

One of the things that sets Sophie apart is her use of routines and rituals to prepare for games. These aren't just habits—they are intentional actions she takes to get into the right mindset and perform at her best. For example, Sophie has a structured kicking routine that she follows before every match. Whether it's a practice session or a high-stakes game, she goes through the same steps: setting up the ball, visualizing the kick, and taking a deep breath before striking it. This routine helps her stay focused and calm, even under pressure.

Sophie's rituals also include mental preparation. Before games, she takes time to visualize herself playing well. She imagines making strong tackles, accurate passes, and successful kicks. This mental imagery helps her build confidence and feel ready to face any challenge on the field.

Routines like Sophie's aren't just for professional athletes—they work for anyone who wants to improve their performance. When you repeat the same actions over and over, your brain learns to associate those actions with success. It's like training your mind to say, "I've done this before, and I can do it again."

For Sophie, her kicking routine helps her block out distractions and focus on the task at hand. By following the same steps every time, she creates a sense of familiarity and control, even in high-pressure situations. This is especially important in rugby, where precision and focus can make the difference between winning and losing.

By breaking her routine into small, manageable steps, Sophie makes a big task—like kicking a goal—feel simple and achievable. Aspiring players can try this too by creating their own routines for tasks like passing, tackling, or even preparing for a game.

Sophie's routines aren't just about physical actions—they also include mental focus. As Canada's captain, she has a lot of responsibility on her shoulders. But instead of letting pressure overwhelm her, Sophie uses her rituals to stay grounded. She talks about how important it is to stay in the moment and focus on what she can control, rather than worrying about things she can't.

One of Sophie's favorite ways to stay focused is by setting small goals for herself during games. For example, she might decide to focus on making strong tackles or supporting her teammates. These mini-goals help her stay motivated and keep her mind on the game.

To create your own pre-game rugby routine, start by identifying the key parts of your preparation, like warming up, stretching, or practicing specific skills. Next, make these actions consistent, repeating them before every game to build familiarity and confidence. Include a moment of mental focus, like visualizing your performance or repeating a positive phrase, to get your mind in the right place. Just like Sophie, following a structured routine can help you feel prepared, calm, and ready to give your best on the field.

Conclusion: Routines and Rituals Bring Game-Day Greatness

Pre-game routines and rituals are powerful tools to help you play your best rugby, no matter your skill level. Just like Sophie de Goede and other professional rugby stars, you can use routines to stay calm, focused, and ready for action. Remember, the key to success is finding habits that work for you.

Take inspiration from some of the quirky pre-game rituals that professional players use to get in the zone. Welsh fly-half Dan Biggar has a unique habit of twitching and adjusting his socks before a kick, which he says helps him concentrate. Irish star Johnny Sexton often uses visualization to prepare for matches, imagining himself making tackles and scoring points. And Springbok captain Siya Kolisi incorporates a moment of prayer and reflection before stepping onto the field, grounding himself in gratitude and focus.

What these routines show is that there's no "one-size-fits-all" approach to pre-game preparation. Whether it's a physical routine like stretching, a symbolic ritual like writing on your tape, or a mental focus technique like visualization, the important thing is consistency. Find small actions or habits that make you feel calm, confident, and ready to play.

When you step onto the field, your routines and rituals will give you a sense of control and readiness. They'll help you manage nerves, block out distractions, and focus on what really matters: the task at hand. So, find what works for you, practice it, and let your rituals become your secret weapon for effective preparation and execution. With a strong routine, you'll be ready to tackle any challenge that comes your way—and find some moments of glory.

3 ACTIVITIES TO HELP YOU WITH YOUR PRE-GAME ROUTINE

#1) Set a Pre-Game Timeline

Decide on a step-by-step schedule leading up to game time and stick to it consistently. For example, arrive at the field 90 minutes early, spend 20 minutes stretching, 30 minutes on skills practice, and 15 minutes on mental preparation. Make this timeline your personal guide for every game day.

Why It Works: Consistency creates familiarity, which reduces game-day anxiety. Following a pre-set timeline ensures you won't feel rushed or disorganized, allowing you to focus on your preparation. A structured routine helps you build confidence by knowing exactly what to expect before each game.

#2) Establish a Consistent Pre-Game Routine Anchor

Choose one activity to consistently start your pre-game routine, like putting on your gear in a specific order, listening to the same song, or tying your boots a certain way. Use this as a "trigger" to kick off the rest of your preparation.

Why It Works: Anchoring your routine with a consistent starting point creates a psychological cue that it's time to focus on preparation. This habit reduces uncertainty and ensures a smooth transition into your pre-game mindset. Over time, this anchor becomes a powerful tool to signal readiness and calm your nerves.

(#3) Designate a Pre-Game Ritual Space

Find a quiet, designated area at the field or in the locker room where you can prepare mentally and physically. Use this space consistently to perform your stretches, mental exercises, or even just take a moment to breathe. Make it your personal "focus zone."

Why It Works: Having a specific space that you associate with preparation helps condition your brain to shift into game mode whenever you enter that environment. This builds a sense of familiarity and control, helping you block out distractions and focus on what matters.

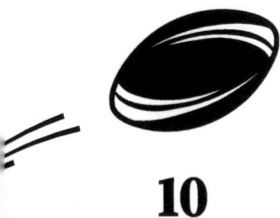

10

POST-MATCH BREAKDOWN:
Reflecting on Your On-Pitch Performance

Imagine this: You just played a tough match against a strong team. Maybe you made some great tackles, but you missed a crucial kick or didn't pass when you should have. Instead of letting those moments pass, performance reflection gives you the chance to learn from them. It's like having a personal coach inside your head, helping you figure out how to do better next time.

Performance reflection is the process of looking back on your game, training session, or even your season to figure out what went well, what didn't, and what you can do better next time. Think of it like watching game film—you're reviewing the action, spotting key plays, and learning from every pass, tackle, and try. It's about understanding your strengths and identifying areas where you can improve, all while keeping a positive and growth-focused mindset.

Performance reflection is important for a few key reasons:

Growth Mindset: Reflection helps you focus on learning and improving, rather than dwelling on mistakes or thinking you're stuck with your current skills.

Confidence Boost: When you recognize your strengths and celebrate your progress, it builds your confidence and motivates you to keep improving.

Problem Solving: By reflecting, you can identify patterns in your play—like why your passes went astray or why you struggled to keep up defensively—and work on specific solutions.

Mental Toughness: Reflection teaches you to handle challenges constructively, which makes you a stronger, more resilient player on and off the field.

How Do the Pros Reflect on Performance?

Professional rugby players know that the small details can make a big difference in their game. That's why reflection is a regular part of their routine. Many players watch video footage of their matches, focusing on specific areas they want to improve. For example, an All Black might review how they approached breakdowns to see if they were effective at winning the ball.

But it's not just about the technical side of the game. Pros often reflect on their mindset during the match. Were they calm under pressure? Did they communicate effectively with teammates? Did they stay focused after making a mistake?

Some players also keep journals to record their thoughts after a game. Writing down what went well, what didn't, and what they'll work on next helps them stay accountable and focused. Players like former Irish fly-half Ronan O'Gara have credited reflection practices like these for helping them reach their peak performance.

How Can You Start Reflecting?

You don't need to be a professional to reflect like one. Here's how you can get started:

Create a Post-Match Routine

Reflection works best when it becomes a habit. After each match, set aside 10-15 minutes to think about your performance. Find a quiet spot where you can focus, or talk it through with a parent, coach, or teammate. The key is to make it a regular part of your rugby routine.

Ask the Right Questions

When reflecting, it's helpful to ask yourself specific questions. Here are a few examples:

- What was my biggest strength in this game?
- What's one thing I'd like to improve next time?
- How did I handle mistakes or challenges during the match?
- Did I stick to my game plan and support my teammates effectively?

By focusing on both the positives and the areas for improvement, you'll get a balanced view of your performance.

Use Tools to Help You Reflect

Some young players find it helpful to keep a rugby journal. After each game, jot down your thoughts and answers to the questions above. You could also create a simple rating system for different aspects of your performance, like tackling, passing, or communication. Over time, you'll start to see patterns that can guide your training.

If your team records games, take the time to watch the footage. Look for moments where you excelled and moments where you could have done better. Watching yourself play can be a powerful way to learn.

Focus on Improvement, Not Perfection

Reflection isn't about beating yourself up over mistakes. Even the best players in the world make errors. Instead, focus on what you can learn and how you can grow. Remember, every game is an opportunity to get better.

Set Goals Based on Your Reflections

Once you've identified areas for improvement, set small, specific goals to work on during training. For example, if you notice that your rucking technique needs work, you might set a goal to practice ruck positioning for 10 minutes at the start of each session. By turning your reflections into actionable steps, you'll see steady progress.

Reflection in Action: An Example

Let's say you're a winger who just finished a tough match. You made a few key runs but missed a tackle that led to a try. During your reflection, you might think about what went well (your speed and positioning) and what didn't (your tackling technique). After talking it through with your coach, you decide to focus on improving your tackle timing during the next week's practice.

The following week, you feel more confident in your tackling because you've worked on it. When the next game comes, you're ready to put your new skills to the test. That's the power of reflection—it turns every match, win or lose, into a chance to grow.

Performance reflection is like a secret weapon for young rugby players. It helps you learn from every game, celebrate your progress, and take control of your development. By creating a reflection habit, you'll build not only your rugby skills but also your confidence and mental toughness.

So, after your next game, take a few minutes to reflect. Ask yourself what went well, what you can improve, and how you'll work on those areas. Over time, you'll discover that reflection isn't just about looking back—it's about moving forward and becoming the best player you can be.

Performance Reflection Science

Thinking about your rugby game after playing isn't just about remembering the best tackles or passes – it's a way to train your brain and improve how you perform. Science shows that reflecting helps your brain's efficiency, keeps your emotions in check, and builds the mental skills needed to succeed.

How Your Brain Helps You Improve:

When you reflect on a game, your brain processes what happened and makes connections to help you improve. For example, the brain's prefrontal cortex is like a coach in your head. It helps you plan, learn from mistakes, and focus. Reflecting after a match strengthens this part of your brain, making it easier to set goals and stay sharp in future games.

Your emotions, like excitement, nervousness, or frustration, come from the amygdala, another part of your brain. If you feel super anxious or angry during a game, it can be harder to focus or make smart decisions. Science shows that reflecting on these feelings after the game helps calm the amygdala and gives the prefrontal cortex a chance to figure out better ways to handle emotions. This is why athletes who reflect often perform better under pressure.

When you review your game – by watching videos or thinking about plays – your brain uses neuroplasticity, its ability to adapt and learn. This means every time you reflect, your brain creates stronger pathways for skills like decision-making, aiming for that perfect pass, or timing your tackles.

Building Mental Skills:

Science also shows that reflecting boosts mental skills like focus, confidence, and problem-solving. It's like lifting weights for your brain! With practice, this helps you make quick, smart choices in the middle of a grueling match.

By combining reflection with what we know about the brain, you can train your mind to help you grow as a player and tackle many challenges on your way to vastly improving your game.

PLAYER PROFILE: ALUN WYN JONES
The Reflective Rugby Warrior

Alun Wyn Jones is one of the greatest rugby players of all time. Born in Wales, Jones has been a powerhouse in the sport for over 15 years. He's played more games for Wales and the British and Irish Lions than anyone else in history. But what makes him so good? It's not just his skills, strength, or leadership—it's his ability to reflect on his performances and constantly improve.

Playing rugby for so many years is tough. Players face injuries, competition, and new challenges every season. Jones's secret weapon has been his ability to look at his past games and figure out how to stay ahead. In an interview with *The Guardian*, Jones admitted he used to be "hot-headed" when he was younger. He sometimes let his emotions get the better of him on the field. By reflecting on those moments, he learned to stay calm under pressure, which helped him become an even better player and captain.

Jones has also talked about how important it is to focus on the basics. He uses reflection to analyze his performance after every game, thinking about his tackling, lineouts, and decision-making. This habit has helped him play smarter, not just harder.

Learning From Setbacks

In rugby, not every game goes as planned. Sometimes, even the best players make mistakes. Instead of getting upset, Jones uses those moments to learn. He told Six Nations Rugby that consistency—being able to perform well game after game—is key. To do this, he reviews his performances and makes small adjustments to his game.

For example, if he misses a tackle, he doesn't just shrug it off. Instead, he asks himself questions like, "Why did I miss that tackle? Was my body position wrong? Was I too slow to react?" By answering these questions, he makes sure he doesn't repeat the same mistake in the next game.

As captain of Wales and the British and Irish Lions, Jones wasn't just responsible for his own game—he had to lead his team, too. Reflection played a big part in how he led. Before games, he would think about how to motivate his teammates and prepare them for the match. After games, he would look at how he communicated with his team and what he could do better as a leader.

Welsh coach Warren Gatland once said that Jones's ability to reflect and adapt made him a great captain. His leadership inspired his teammates to work harder and perform better.

Learnings From Alun Wyn Jones

So, what can aspiring rugby players like you learn from Alun Wyn Jones? First, remember that every game is a chance to get better. After your matches, take some time to think about how you played.

What did you do well? What could you improve? Write it down or talk about it with your coach or teammates.

Second, don't be afraid to learn from your mistakes. Even the best players mess up sometimes. What matters is how you respond. Use those mistakes as opportunities to grow.

Finally, stay focused on the basics. Just like Jones, mastering the fundamentals of rugby—like tackling, passing, and decision-making—can make a huge difference in your game.

Alun Wyn Jones shows us that reflection is one of the most powerful tools in rugby. It's helped him stay at the top of the sport for over a decade, and it can help you, too. By thinking about your performance, learning from mistakes, and always looking for ways to improve, you can become the best player—and teammate— you can be.

Just remember: even legends like Alun Wyn Jones started where you are now. With hard work and a reflective mindset, you will achieve great things, too.

Conclusion: Post-Match Reflection for Young Ruggers

As an aspiring rugby player, it's easy to focus on big moments— scoring a try, making a powerful tackle, or missing a kick—but the real magic lies in what you do after the match. Reflection is the hidden superpower of the best players in the game, a tool that turns every experience into an opportunity to grow. By looking back on your performance and thinking about what went well and what didn't, you can set yourself up for future success.

Reflecting isn't about pointing out flaws or beating yourself up over mistakes; it's about learning and improving. Every match, win or lose, is a chance to get better. When you reflect, you train your brain to focus on solutions rather than problems. Did you feel nervous before kickoff? Did your passes go astray? Did you support your teammates effectively? Each question leads to insights that can sharpen your game.

Take it from someone like Alun Wyn Jones, a rugby legend who used reflection to rise to the top of the sport. Jones analyzed every match, learning from both victories and setbacks. He didn't shy away from mistakes but used them as stepping stones to improvement. His ability to reflect and adjust made him not just a better player, but a great leader.

The good news? You don't have to be a pro to get started. Create a simple post-match routine. Spend 10-15 minutes thinking about your game or talking it through with a coach, parent, or teammate. Focus on what went well and what could be improved. If you missed a tackle, ask yourself why. If you made a great pass, think about how you can replicate that.

Some players find it helpful to keep a rugby journal, jotting down their thoughts and setting goals for the next game. Others review match footage to see where they excelled and where they struggled. Whatever method you choose, the key is consistency. Make reflection a habit, and you'll start to see the difference in your performance.

Above all, remember that perfection isn't the goal—progress is. Even the best players in the world have bad games. What sets them apart is how they use those experiences to grow. So, after your next match, take the time to reflect. Celebrate your strengths, learn from your mistakes, and focus on how you can improve.

With a reflective mindset, you're not just playing rugby—you're building a foundation for success. Every match is a stepping stone to becoming the player and teammate you dream of being. Embrace the process, and watch your game reach new heights.

4 ACTIVITIES TO HELP WITH PERFORMANCE REFLECTION

#1 Video Review Sessions

Watch footage of your games (if available). Focus on one aspect of your performance, like defense, passing, or positioning. Note key moments—good and bad—and consider how you could improve. If you don't have video access, visualize the game in your mind and walk through the key plays.

Why It Works: Seeing yourself play provides a different perspective than relying on memory alone. You can catch details you might've missed in the moment and analyze your decisions. This visual feedback is powerful for making corrections and reinforcing effective techniques.

#2 Post-Match Journaling

After each match or training session, spend 10-15 minutes writing in a journal. Divide the page into three sections: "What Went Well," "What Could Be Better," and "Goals for Next Time."

Reflect on specific moments, like successful tackles, missed opportunities, or teamwork. Be honest but also focus on positives and ways to grow.

Why It Works: Journaling creates a structured way to think through your performance, helping you identify patterns over time. Writing things down strengthens memory and helps your brain process experiences better. It also builds self-awareness and makes your reflections actionable, which leads to steady improvement.

#3 Teammate Feedback Circles

After a game or training, gather with a small group of teammates to share reflections. Each player mentions one thing they did well, one area they want to improve, and one positive observation about a teammate. Keep the atmosphere supportive and constructive.

Why It Works: Feedback from others helps you see your performance through different eyes. Hearing constructive insights from teammates strengthens trust and provides ideas for growth. The activity also fosters a team culture of accountability and support, which benefits everyone.

#4 Mistake Mapping

After a game, list any mistakes or challenges you faced, like missed tackles or dropped passes. For each one, write down what caused it and one way to address it in training. For example, if fatigue causes a mistake, focus on conditioning drills.

Why It Works: Mistake mapping shifts your mindset from frustration to problem-solving. By analyzing and addressing mistakes constructively, you'll grow faster and reduce the likelihood of repeating them. It also strengthens your ability to handle setbacks mentally.

CONCLUSION:
Building Your Mental Fitness Toolkit for Rugby Success

Rugby is not just a game of strength, speed, and skill—it is a test of mental toughness, resilience, and adaptability. Throughout this book, you have explored the essential components of mental fitness: overcoming mental blocks, building emotional regulation, harnessing the power of visualization, developing a growth mindset, strengthening resilience and grit, practicing mindfulness, setting clear goals, using positive self-talk, creating effective rituals and routines, and reflecting on performance. These tools are not just ideas; they are actionable strategies that will help you become a stronger, more confident, and more composed rugby player.

Why Mental Fitness Matters in Rugby

Rugby is one of the most physically and mentally demanding sports. Every match requires you to push past pain, handle setbacks, and stay composed under pressure. Whether it's keeping your focus when your team is trailing late in the game, bouncing back from a missed tackle, or preparing mentally for a tough opponent, your mindset determines how well you perform.

Legendary players like Jonny Wilkinson and Richie McCaw were not just known for their technical skills but for their exceptional mental strength. Wilkinson's pre-kick visualization and meticulous routines helped him stay composed under pressure, while

McCaw's relentless grit and ability to adapt to any challenge made him one of the greatest captains in rugby history. These players understood that their mental approach was just as important as their physical training.

Mental fitness is not just about rugby—it's about preparing for life. The same skills that help you stay calm under pressure in a game will help you manage stress in school, face challenges in relationships, and pursue personal goals with confidence and resilience.

Mental Fitness in Action: Learning from the Pros

Professional rugby players know that mental training is just as important as physical training. Take Siya Kolisi—his journey from a tough childhood to global success was fueled by mental resilience, self-belief, and the ability to stay composed under pressure. He used setbacks as motivation and remained focused on his goals, proving that mental strength is a key ingredient for success.

Another great example is Dan Carter, whose ability to stay mentally composed allowed him to make split-second decisions under pressure. His visualization techniques and game-day routines ensured he was prepared for every match. These players don't leave their mental game to chance—they train their minds just like they train their bodies.

How to Apply Mental Fitness to Your Game

Success in rugby isn't just about training harder—it's about training smarter. That means developing the mental habits that will keep you focused, resilient, and confident. Here's how you can apply the principles in this book to your game:

- Struggling with pre-game nerves? Practice mindfulness and breathing exercises to stay calm before kickoff.

- Overthinking mistakes? Use positive self-talk and performance reflection to learn from errors without dwelling on them.

- Lacking confidence? Develop a growth mindset by focusing on progress rather than perfection.

- Feeling overwhelmed in tough matches? Build resilience by embracing challenges as opportunities to grow.
- Want to improve focus? Create a game-day routine that mentally prepares you to perform at your best.

Consistency is Key

Just like improving your passing, tackling, or kicking, developing mental fitness takes consistent effort. You wouldn't expect to get stronger in the gym after one workout, and the same applies to your mental skills. Incorporate these strategies into your daily routine and be patient with yourself as you grow.

Start small. Pick one or two areas to focus on and gradually build from there. Maybe you begin by setting clear goals for each match or practicing visualization before training sessions. Over time, these small changes will have a huge impact on your performance.

The Bigger Picture

Mental fitness isn't just about winning games—it's about becoming a stronger, more resilient person. The skills you develop through rugby will help you in every aspect of life. Whether you're dealing with school stress, handling personal setbacks, or striving toward your dreams, the mental tools you've learned will serve you well.

The rugby journey is filled with highs and lows. There will be games where everything clicks and matches where nothing goes your way. What matters most is how you respond. A mentally strong player doesn't let one bad game define them—they learn, adapt, and come back stronger.

A Call to Action

As you finish this book and step back onto the pitch, remember: mental fitness is your greatest asset. It is what will separate you from other players. Reflect on the strategies you've learned and make a commitment to practicing them every day. Celebrate your progress, no matter how small, and embrace challenges as opportunities to grow.

The best rugby players aren't the ones who never fail—they're the ones who never stop improving. You have everything you need to succeed—now it's time to put it into action. Stay committed, trust the process, and let your mental fitness take your game to the next level. Rugby is more than a sport—it's an opportunity to grow, to learn, and to become the best version of yourself, now hit the pitch and go get it!

ACKNOWLEDGEMENTS

This book would not have been possible without the support, guidance, and inspiration of many incredible people.

To **Simon Stringer**, thank you for capturing the spirit of the game through your photography. Your talent brings rugby to life in a way that words cannot.

To **Sophie de Goede**, your leadership on and off the pitch is an inspiration. Thank you for your support of this book and for being a shining example of what it means to lead with strength and integrity.

To the **Williams Lake Rustlers**, thank you for fostering such a welcoming and inclusive rugby community. Once a Rustler, always a Rustler.

To the **Kamloops Raiders Rugby Club**, your support and direction came at a time I truly needed it. Rugby is more than a game—it's a family. One in, all in.

And to my father, **Mike Levitt**, thank you for introducing me to the beautiful game of rugby and for the countless lessons you've taught me, both on and off the pitch. Your passion for the sport and unwavering support mean the world to me.

ABOUT THE AUTHOR

COLE LEVITT:

Cole Levitt has dedicated his career to supporting the well-being of children and youth, as a coach, an educator, and now as a child and family therapist. With 25+ years of rugby experience, at many levels, Cole possesses a deep understanding of sports psychology and the significant impact of mental mindset on a rugby player's athletic performance.

His journey through the rugby world, combined with the therapeutic work he does with young athletes, has equipped him with invaluable insights into the challenges young ruggers face and the strategies they can employ to overcome their mental barriers.

As a therapist, Cole combines his athletic experience with professional expertise in child development, sports psychology, education and mental health. This unique combination allows him to offer an insightful and strategic approach to creating a strong mental mindset, tailored specifically to young, competitive rugby players. His dedication to helping young rugby players reach their fullest potential is the driving force behind this book.

In "Mental Fitness for Young Rugby Players," Cole shares practical activities, proven strategies, and valuable insights designed to empower young rugby players to mentally thrive and master their mental game.

Sources

Above the Rim: Rising Breaking the Line: Identifying and Fending Off Mental Blocks

Beilock, S. L., & Carr, T. H. (2001). *On the fragility of skilled performance: What governs choking under pressure?* Journal of Experimental Psychology: General, 130(4), 701–725. https://doi.org/10.1037/0096-3445.130.4.701

H Han D, H Kim J, S Lee Y, Joeng Bae S, Jin Bae S, J Kim H, Y Sim M, H Sung Y, Kyoon Lyoo I. Influence of temperament and anxiety on athletic performance. J Sports Sci Med. 2006 Sep 1;5(3):381-9. PMID: 24353455; PMCID: PMC3842138.

Hughes, G. (Director). (2021). *Big Boys Don't Cry.* RSA Films.

Joe Marler discusses battle with depression and goes on journey to rebuild his mental health in Sky Sports' Big Boys Don't Cry. (n.d.). Sky Sports. https://www.skysports.com/rugby-union/news/12321/12303342/joe-marler-discusses-battle-with-depression-and-goes-on-journey-to-rebuild-his-mental-health-in-sky-sports-big-boys-dont-cry

Joe Marler stars in Sky Sports documentary exploring the matter of Mental Health. (2021). Skygroup. sky. https://www.skygroup.sky/article/joe-marler-stars-in-sky-sports-documentary-exploring-the-matter-of-mental-health

Phelps, E. A., & LeDoux, J. E. (2005). *Contributions of the amygdala to emotion processing: From animal models to human behavior.* Neuron, 48(2), 175-187. https://doi.org/10.1016/j.neuron.2005.09.025

Raisey, J. (2020, September 23). *Marler's mission to break rugby's mental health taboo.* Rugbypass. com; RugbyPass. https://www.rugbypass.com/news/marlers-mission-to-break-rugbys-mental-health-taboo-marler-england/

Head in the Game: Emotional Regulation for the Pitch

Campo M, Champely S, Lane AM, Rosnet E, Ferrand C, Louvet B. Emotions and performance in rugby. J Sport Health Sci. 2019 Nov;8(6):595-600. doi:10.1016/j.jshs.2016.05.007. Epub 2016 May 25. PMID: 31720073; PMCID: PMC6834972.

Deep Dive with Ali Abdaal. (2023, October 12). *Rugby Legend: "This Mindset Will Make You A Champion In Anything" Dan Carter.* YouTube. https://www.youtube.com/watch?v=zOio-wUP46A

From chokers to champs: All Blacks legend's secrets to success. (2023, July 17). Forbes Australia. https://www.forbes.com.au/covers/leadership/all-black-dan-carter-on-dealing-with-pressure/

How focusing on the process not the outcome can help us to manage stress. (2015). Barberassociates.co.uk. https://www.barberassociates.co.uk/blog/how-focusing-on-the-process-not-the-outcome-can-help-us-to-manage-stress

Martinent, G., Ledos, S., Ferrand, C., Campo, M., & Nicolas, M. (2015). Athletes' regulation of emotions experienced during competition: A naturalistic video-assisted study. *Sport, Exercise, and Performance Psychology*, 4(3), 188–205. https://doi.org/10.1037/spy0000037

McEwen, B. S. (2007). Physiology and neurobiology of stress and adaptation: Central role of the brain. *Physiological Reviews*, 87(3), 873-904. Retrieved from https://doi.org/10.1152/physrev.00041.2006

Miller, E. K., & Cohen, J. D. (2001). An integrative theory of prefrontal cortex function. *Annual Review of Neuroscience*, 24(1), 167-202. Retrieved from https://doi.org/10.1146/annurev.neuro.24.1.167

Miruna-Ioana Girtu. (2023, September 26). Performing Under Pressure: Sporting Legend Dan Carter Shares His Playbook With Entrepreneurs. *Forbes.* https://www.forbes.com/sites/mirunagirtu/2023/09/26/performing-under-pressure-sporting-legend-dan-carter-shares-his-playbook-with-entrepreneurs

World Rugby. (2022, October 3). *Dan Carter and Portia Woodman discuss the importance of mental preparation ahead of RWC2021.* YouTube. https://www.youtube.com/watch?v=yiYa0XElgSs

Mental Maul: Visualizing Victory on the Rugby Field

Binner, A. (2020, December 2). *Exclusive! Rugby ace Portia Woodman on her mission for double gold in 2021.* Olympics.com; International Olympic Committee. https://olympics.com/en/news/interview-portia-woodman-rugby-double-gold-2021?utm_

Brian Moylett. (2021, December 4). *Portia Woodman | The Off-Field Rugby Pod Ep #20.* YouTube. https://www.youtube.com/watch?v=pInzKXFLjb4

Evans, L., Jones, L., & Mullen, R. (2004). An imagery intervention during the competitive season with an elite rugby union player. *The Sport Psychologist*, 18(3), 252-271.

Guillot, A., & Collet, C. (2008). Construction of the motor image: A review and theoretical framework. *Behavioral and Brain Sciences*, 31(2), 227-247.

Parnabas, V. A., & Mahamood, Y. (2012). Anxiety and imagery of green space among athletes. *British Journal of Arts and Social Sciences*, 4(1), 67-72.

Player-Development-Project. (2016, March 24). *The Power of Positive Visualisation - Player Development Project.* Player Development Project. https://playerdevelopmentproject.com/the-power-of-positive-visualisation/

Predoiu, R.,Predoiu, A., Mitrache, G., Firănescu, M., Cosma, G., Dinuță, G., & Bucuroiu, R. A. (2020). Visualisation techniques in sport – The mental road map for success. *Discobolul-Physical Education, Sport & Kinetotherapy Journal*, 59(3).

Stephen, F. A., Ermalyn, L. P., Yasmin, M. B., Louise, L. J. D., & Juvenmile, T. B. . (2022). A Voyage into the Visualization of Athletic Performances: A Review. *American Journal of Multidisciplinary Research and Innovation*, 1(3), 105–109. https://doi.org/10.54536/ajmri.v1i3.479

Through the Phases: Elevating Your Game with a Growth Mindset

Dweck, C. S. (2006). *Mindset: The new psychology of success.*

Dweck, C. S. (2009). *Mindsets: Developing talent through a growth mindset. Olympic coach*, 21(1), 4-7.

Dweck, C. S. (2016). Developing talent through a growth mindset. *OLYMPIC COACH*, 21(1).

Hatchett, L. (2023, November 3). *What the Springbok Mindset Can Teach Us*. Lewis Hatchett. https://lewishatchett.com/what-the-springbok-mindset-can-teach-us/

Kolisi Foundation. (n.d.). *Home*. Kolisi Foundation. Retrieved January 29, 2025, from https://kolisifoundation.org/

Mweli, S. (2023, October 2). *From Humble Beginnings to Rugby Legend: The Inspiring Tale of Siya Kolisi*. Medium. https://medium.com/@siphesihle112.mweli/from-humble-beginnings-to-rugby-legend-the-inspiring-tale-of-siya-kolisi-e3c38e78431e

Vivier, T. L. (2023, October 10). *Siya Kolisi Chats Mental Mindset Going into Rugby World Cup*. *Good Things Guy*. https://www.goodthingsguy.com/sport/siya-kolisi-chats-mental-mindset-going-into-rugby-world-cup/

Tackling Tough Times: Building Resilience on and off the Pitch

Aggarwal, E. (2024, October 27). *Facing Internet Backlash, Ilona Maher Reflects on the Weight of Expectations: "Struggled With My Mental Health."* EssentiallySports. https://www.essentiallysports.com/us-sports-news-olympics-news-rugby-news-facing-internet-backlash-ilona-maher-reflects-on-the-weight-of-expectations-struggled-with-my-mental-health

Davidson, R. J., & McEwen, B. S. (2012). Social influences on neuroplasticity: Stress and interventions to promote well-being. *Nature Neuroscience*, 15(5), 689–695.

Duckworth, A. (2016). *Grit: The power of passion and perseverance*. Scribner/Simon & Schuster.

Duckworth, A. L., Peterson, C., Matthews, M. D., & Kelly, D. R. (2007). Grit: Perseverance and passion for long-term goals. *Journal of Personality and Social Psychology*, 92(6), 1087-1101. https://doi.org/10.1037/0022-3514.92.6.1087

Mendizabal, B. (2024). The relationship between athletes' grit, mental toughness, and sport resilience. *Physical Education of Students*, 28(4), 188–194. https://doi.org/10.15561/20755279.2024.0401

News, A. R. (2023, March 21). *Ilona Maher to miss remainder of World Sevens Series*. Americas Rugby News. https://www.americasrugbynews.com/2023/03/20/ilona-maher-to-miss-remainder-of-world-sevens-series/

People. (2024). *Ilona Maher says adjusting to viral fame was "hard" — but working with sports psychologist helped (Exclusive)*. People.com. https://people.com/2024-olympics-star-ilona-maher-adjusting-viral-fame-was-hard-exclusive-8692455

People. (2024). *Ilona Maher says her Olympic bronze medal 'felt like a gold': 'We call it rose gold' (Exclusive)*. People. https://people.com/ilona-maher-says-olympic-bronze-medal-felt-like-a-gold-exclusive-8727418

Clearing the Ruck: Using Mindfulness for Focus and Performance

Birrer, Daniel & Röthlin, Philipp & Morgan, Gareth. (2012). *Mindfulness to Enhance Athletic Performance: Theoretical Considerations and Possible Impact Mechanisms*. Mindfulness. 3. 10.1007/s12671-012-0109-2.

Kabat-Zinn, J. (2013). *Mindfulness for beginners: Reclaiming the present moment—and your life.* Shambhala Publications.

Myall K, Montero-Marin J, Gorczynski P, *et al.* Effect of mindfulness-based programmes on elite athlete mental health: a systematic review and meta-analysis. *British Journal of Sports Medicine* 2023;57:99-108.

New Year, New Options This year, Johnny Sexton is... (n.d.). https://www.facebook.com/watch/?v=895969722743330

O'Dea, A. J. (2021, January 30). *How mindfulness helps Johnny Sexton through the bad days.* OffTheBall. https://www.offtheball.com/rugby/johnn-sexton-mindfulness-1143122

Sapuppo W, Giacconi D, Monda V, Messina A, Allocca S, Chieffi S, Ricci M, Villano I, Saccenti D, Mineo CM, Boltri M, Monda M, Di Maio G, Monda A, La Marra M. Functional Characteristics and Coping Strategies among Rugby Athletes: A Cluster Analysis Approach. J Pers Med. 2024 Mar 9;14(3):292. doi: 10.3390/jpm14030292. PMID: 38541034; PMCID: PMC10970941.

"There's 80,000 people watching... it's like a war" - Johnny Sexton. (2024). *RTE Radio.* Urn:clipper:22441572

Eyes on the Try Line: Aligning Your Goals with Your Training and Play

Associated Press. (n.d.). *France wins rugby sevens gold at Paris 2024 Olympics, ending Fiji's dominance.* Retrieved from https://apnews.com/article/olympics-2024-france-dupont-rugby-sevens-cbd70cdb6235787b082af3af98bde920

Kingston, K. M., & Hardy, L. (1997). Effects of different types of goals on processes that support performance. *The Sport Psychologist,* 11(3), 277-293.

Locke EA, Latham GP. Building a practically useful theory of goal setting and task motivation. A 35-year odyssey. Am Psychol. 2002 Sep;57(9):705-17. doi: 10.1037//0003-066x.57.9.705. PMID: 12237980.

Lofgren, J. (2020, April 17). The neuroscience behind setting goals. Carrick Institute https://carrickinstitute.com/the-neuroscience-behind-setting-goals/

Olympics.com. (n.d.). *Antoine Dupont aims for rugby sevens glory at Paris 2024.* Retrieved from https://olympics.com/en/news/antoine-dupont-interview-vancouver-7s-paris-2024-rugby-france

Reeve, J., & Lee, W. (2012). Neuroscience and human motivation. *The Oxford handbook of human motivation,* 365-380.

RugbyPass. (n.d.). *Antoine Dupont - Player Profile.* Retrieved from https://www.rugbypass.com/players/antoine-dupont

Salamone JD, Correa M. The mysterious motivational functions of mesolimbic dopamine. Neuron. 2012 Nov 8;76(3):470-85. doi: 10.1016/j.neuron.2012.10.021. PMID: 23141060; PMCID: PMC4450094. \

Ultimate Rugby. (n.d.). *Antoine Dupont - Player Profile.* Retrieved from https://www.ultimaterugby.com/antoine-dupont

Gaining Advantage: Keeping Positive Self Talk in Play

Crisis Talk. (n.d.). *Post-rugby reflections on mental health and self-compassion.* Retrieved from https://talk.crisisnow.com/former-professional-rugby-player-joe-williams-on-self-compassion-and-intergenerational-trauma/

Hatzigeorgiadis, A., Zourbanos, N., Galanis, E., & Theodorakis, Y. (2011). Self-talk and sports performance: A meta-analysis. *Perspectives on Psychological Science, 6*(4), 348-356.

Kim, J., Kwon, J. H., Kim, J., Kim, E. J., Kim, H. E., Kyeong, S., & Kim, J. (2021). The effects of positive or negative self-talk on the alteration of brain functional connectivity by performing cognitive tasks. *Scientific Reports, 11*(1). https://doi.org/10.1038/s41598-021-94328-9

Rugby World. (n.d.). *2003 World Cup Final: How Jonny Wilkinson's drop goal secured victory.* Retrieved from https://www.rugbyworld.com/tournaments/rugby-world-cup/2003-world-cup-final-how-johnny-wilkinsons-drop-goal-won-it-77671

The Independent. (n.d.). *Jonny Wilkinson's mental game: Insights into his strategies.* Retrieved from https://www.the-independent.com/life-style/health-and-families/jonny-wilkinson-england-rugby-union-australia-england-rugby-b2264218.html

The High Performance Podcast. (n.d.). *Jonny Wilkinson's mental approach to rugby.* Retrieved from https://www.thehighperformancepodcast.com/podcast/jonny-wilkinson

Theodorakis, Y., Weinberg, R., Natsis, P., Douma, I., & Kazakas, P. (2000). The effects of motivational versus instructional self-talk on improving motor performance. The Sport Psychologist, 14(3), 253-271.

Tod, D., Hardy, J., & Oliver, E. (2011). Effects of self-talk: A systematic review. *Journal of Sport and Exercise Psychology, 33*(5), 666-687.

Try-Time: Rituals and Routines for Gameday Greatness

Aedelhard. (n.d.). *Sophie de Goede: Celebrating rugby royalty in Canada.* Aedelhard. Retrieved from https://aedelhard.com/blogs/stories/sophie-de-goede-celebrating-rugby-royalty-in-canada

Brooks, A. W., Schroeder, J., Risen, J. L., Gino, F., Galinsky, A. D., Norton, M. I., & Schweitzer, M. E. (2016). Don't stop believing: Rituals improve performance by decreasing anxiety. *Organizational Behavior and Human Decision Processes, 137*(1), 71-85.

Coast Reporter. (n.d.). *Canada captain Sophie de Goede turns heads ahead of Rugby World Cup in New Zealand.* Coast Reporter. Retrieved from https://www.coastreporter.net/national-sports/canada-captain-sophie-de-goede-turns-heads-ahead-of-rugby-world-cup-in-new-zealand-5907270

Hobson, N. M., Bonk, D., & Inzlicht, M. (2017). Rituals decrease the neural response to performance failure. *PeerJ, 5*, e3363. https://doi.org/10.7717/peerj.3363

Hobson, N. M., et al. (2017). "Rituals reduce anxiety by imposing structure." *Current Directions in Psychological Science.*

McCann, S. (2008). Routines, rituals, and performing under pressure. *Olympic Coach, 20*(2), 14-15.

RugbyPass. (n.d.). Sophie de Goede: *"We are peaking at the right time."* RugbyPass. Retrieved from https://www.rugbypass.com/news/sophie-de-goede-we-are-peaking-at-the-right-time/

Rugby World. (n.d.). *Sophie de Goede and a Canadian rugby dynasty.* Rugby World. Retrieved from https://www.rugbyworld.com/featured/sophie-de-goede-and-a-canadian-rugby-dynasty-146927

Post-Match Breakdown: Reflecting on Your On-Pitch Performance

BBC Sport. (2019, April 5). *Wales captain Alun Wyn Jones focused on World Cup amid future questions.* Retrieved from https://www.bbc.com/sport/rugby-union/47830666

Budnarowska, M., & Turek, K. (2020). Neuroplasticity and motor learning in sport activity. *European Journal of Physical Education and Sport Science,* 6(8), 40–52. Retrieved from https://efsupit.ro/images/stories/august2020/Art%20318.pdf

Chow, G. M., & Luzzeri, M. (2019). Post-event reflection: A tool to facilitate self-awareness, self-monitoring, and self-regulation in athletes. *Journal of Sport Psychology in Action,* 10(2), 106-118.

MacIntyre, T. E., Igou, E. R., Campbell, M. J., Moran, A. P., & Matthews, J. (2014). Metacognition and action: a new pathway to understanding social and cognitive aspects of expertise in sport. *Frontiers in Psychology,* 5. https://doi.org/10.3389/fpsyg.2014.01155

Rees, P. (2019, March 17). *Alun Wyn Jones: Pain-defying warrior needed for more Wales battles.* The Guardian. Retrieved from https://www.theguardian.com/sport/2019/mar/17/alun-wyn-jones-pain-defying-warrior-needed-for-more-wales-battles

Six Nations Rugby. (2020). *Alun Wyn Jones: A champion in three decades.* Retrieved from https://www.sixnationsrugby.com/en/m6n/news/alun-wyn-jones-a-champion-in-three-decades

The Telegraph. (2021, August 9). *Forget Maro Itoje and Eben Etzebeth – Alun Wyn Jones left his mark on Lions history.* Retrieved from https://www.telegraph.co.uk/rugby-union/2021/08/09/forget-maro-itoje-eben-etzebeth-alun-wyn-jones-left-mark-lions

Printed in Dunstable, United Kingdom